The Life and Times of
Francie Nichol
of South Shields

The Life and Times of Francie Nichol of South Shields

by

Joe Robinson

London . George Allen & Unwin Ltd
Ruskin House . Museum Street

First published in 1975

© Joe Robinson 1975

ISBN 0 04 920042 9

Printed in Great Britain
in 11 point Baskerville type
by Willmer Brothers Limited, Birkenhead

To
Judy, Dominic,
Ngaire and Daniel

Introduction

James Nichol, a bricklayer, was honest and hard-working when sober. Elizabeth Billclough was pleasant to look at, and quiet. Equally honest but harder-working than her husband, she was always sober because she could never afford the luxury of an alcoholic drink. Together they made fourteen children, seven boys and seven girls. Of these, only six girls survived: JaneAnne, Alice, Nellie, Lily, Lizzie, and Francie.

On a Saturday in the year 1891, JaneAnne, the Nichols' eldest daughter, was married to Jim Kilcaldy, a Scot by descent and a Geordie by birth. The following day, the Sunday, the bride's mother decamped with her remaining five children. Bessie had often thought about leaving her husband and had even gone so far as to threaten. But this time she had no qualms left.

Dinner was being served. In those days Father was the undisputed lord no matter how small the manor, and however frugal the fare. Ritualistic discipline was the order, the man of the house at all times presiding, with the woman giving at least a show of support. No backchat here. Not even from the woman, let alone the children. Precocity was played out in the street with other kids. Spend it there or on each other but never ever dare challenge Father even with so much as a defiant glance. Their grandfather and great-grandfather had been the same. It was the law of nature. Women could not reproach or reason with their men—too much of that and they would get a touch of the old leather. They would expect their own sons to grow up and be men who acted likewise. When all was said and done, women were for the convenience of the men, and children were the by-products. Washing, cooking, cleaning, rearing and being thankful for it, was their lot. Better than the workhouse. And that, too often, *was* the only alternative.

Dinner was now on the table.

'What the bloody hell does she think she's doin'?'

Lizzie had put her finger in the rabbit pie and started eating before the roaring drunken father had gathered up his knife and fork.

'I'll murder the little bastard!'

Mother tried to restrain Father. But it was no good. The table was over, the food spilled and flung to the floor. The children scattered and Mother ended up with the carving knife held to her throat.

'As for you, ye interferin' bitch, I'll slit your bloody gullet when that big pointer gets to twelve!'

Jimmy Nichol had knocked her about a bit from time to time, of course, but nothing like this before. Normally she never raised her voice in protest or her hand in defence, but this time she was very, very frightened.

'Please no, Jimmy. I'm very sorry. You might be sorry afterwards. She's only a bairn. She's only four.'

'Shut your mouth, woman, or I'll do you in right now.'

Meanwhile all but Francie, who was too young to realise what was going on, had fled to the landing outside. Alice ran to seek JaneAnne and Jim Kilcaldy who immediately returned with her, flung open the door and wrested the gully from Father. In the ensuing scuffle he knocked his drunken father-in-law to the floor and would probably have killed him had it not been for Mother's pleas. 'No! No . . . leave him be! Leave him be! He didn't really mean it. He was just upset. Our Lizzie had been very naughty and should have known better. They've all been told before. They know he doesn't like. . . .'

'Come on Ma, you're coming with us. Get Francie and I'll bring your stuff. What d'ye want? These chairs? Here JaneAnne! Put those over there in a box or something. I'll get everything else.'

'No, no, you mustn't. I want nothing. Leave them. You can't do this to him. They belong to him. It's all his. He's worked hard for everything, for the little he's got.'

'Don't worry, Ma, he won't hurt you. Take the lot. The sod's lucky to be left in one piece.'

Jim, who had also had a few drinks, started angrily towards the glowering, threatening father. Mother cried out, 'If you harm him, or even touch him again, I'll brain you, Jim Kilcaldy. I'll come with you, but you must leave him alone.'

'You must be daft, Ma. Howay then, get little Francie. We're goin'. Leave that bugger to stew in his own juice. He'll never get another like you.

'And that's for bloody sure!' he shouted in Nichol's face.

Francie Nichol, born on 18 April 1889 in South Shields, was now two years old.

1

Well, we certainly couldn't all stay at Jim and JaneAnne's for long. They only had one room themselves in Heron Street, and they had to cook, sleep, wash and do everythin' else in that. Poor souls. . . . What a way to start their marriage. However, they couldn't complain really. There was many a lot worse off than them and they knew it.

Me mother wasn't a one to sit down and start cryin'. She kept herself always busy for us kids and never had no time for anythin' else. Except if somebody was needin' help. Then she would do whatever she could to help them and they would be grateful for it. In no time at all she got us a little place—not much, but quite canny, and we stayed there till we got worselves put right. There was nowt in it of course. Just a bare room. But it was fairly dry where we used to lie. For the first two weeks we just slept on the bare boards but little by little we all got beds, after a fashion. Me mam was working in the kipper factory where she had worked all her life, packin' herrin'. When she finished there at the end of the day, she would ask the man if there was any broken ones she could have to keep for hersel'. She would then make them up nice and go and sell them for a few extra coppers.

Straw was cheap and the bigger girls and me mam sewed sackin' around it to make comfy little beds. She got some bricks from some of the old houses they were pullin' down and we built a table. And when it was scrubbed and varnished with a bit of cloth on it, ye wouldn't know the difference. Next she got hold of two wooden forms, like long crackets or stools, one at each side.

Naturally we had no proper eatin' things at first, so we made do with what we could get. Milk tins were good because they had no sharp edges. The milk was nearly as cheap as water. It wasn't Nestlés or anythin' like that, just the dried milk ye could buy at the market.

11

After a while we got on champion. The older girls were gettin' bits of char jobs and that, and me mother was buildin' up a little business bringin' in laundry and washin' for mebbes twopence or threepence a load. Hand-wringin' with an old mangle she picked up, and so on. Ye could put stuff to sell in your windows at that time and she used to make ginger beer, cinder toffee, vinegar and a few buns, sell it, and get a few more shillin's. Then we got cups. The oldest ones had the cups with handles and then when they got a better one, they used to pass them down till we all got one. Then knives and forks to go around. Me mother really did her best to make things nice for we. Folks thought well of her because she worked so hard for us kids and because she was so clean and willin', and so they would keep comin' back bringin' their cleanin' jobs.

She often worked through the night as well as durin' the day and she never got so much as a single penny out of me father. Her job at Woodhouse's kipper factory was only a seasonal one. Usually June to August when they were bringin' in piles of good big herrin'. In summer she got her stock in ready for the winter. Big drums of flour, sugar, tea and such like, and a couple of pairs of shoes each for the kids where she could, because she knew every winter would be a hard one with only the washin' to rely on.

Even though he caused me mother so much trouble, she would never have ye say anythin' about me father. It took her all her time to say 'damn', and if anybody had a right to be a sinner it should have been her, because so help me God she had an awful life. She did that. Every now and then he would find out where we were livin'. Always we had only one room. We changed places umpteen times to try and get away from him, but he was crafty and would follow us kids home from school. Me mother daren't keep us off altogether. We weren't there hardly ever as it was. I was off at least two or three times a week for the hawkin', sellin' fish and greens, that is. I left school when I was twelve, in standard two, I think. Mind, I wasn't much of a scholar anyway. I could do sums but I couldn't write them, and I suppose that's what really matters.

We would just be sittin' down to tea when he would sud-

denly come crashin' through the door. Me mother was terrified
of him. He would knock her into a corner and she would just
stay there, not knowing what to do. Wor Alice, who was a big
strappin' girl, was the only one who dared to stand up to him.
But sometimes even she couldn't handle him and he'd soon sort
her out as well. One night when I was about four or five, he
had come in and started his antics, smashin' up the furniture,
bashin' me mother and upsettin' the table with all the food on.
He would always do that before he went out. Well, this time I
remember he says to me mother, 'Come here and give's a kiss. I
don't know, you think I don't love you but I do as surely as the
shore dashes on the waves.'

He was as soft as shit really. Alice rushed up to him and gave
him a big shove. He fell in the bath of water that I was in and
there was murder on. It took him so long to get out because he
was so drunk and he'd got his arse jammed in the bath next to
me. It was a kind of a rain tub that had been sawed down. Me
mother ran out and hid outside until he'd went. I think he felt
a bit of a fool and didn't come around for quite a long time
after that. It's a good job the water hadn't been boilin'. He
certainly was.

I don't know why but that reminds me of the only time I
ever saw me mother's father. He was old and white and sittin'
in a chair. I was frightened and never wanted to go back
again. I didn't know it was him at the time, I must have been
very young. I never saw me father's people but I once saw me
grandmother. It was when she was laid out on the table waitin'
for the people to come and take her away. There were three
big rolls of bacon hangin' up above her head. I fancy they were
fairly well off, comparisonly speakin' that is.

By, we had some cold days as well. Not that that was much.
It was the damp that used to get into your bones. It must have
got into me poor mother's. And I don't think it ever properly
got out. It didn't bother me of course, I was a growin' girl and
I was very hardy. I used to get fuel whenever I could to try
and keep the place warm for me mother. You could see the
cold comin' out of her face and in her hands. Her hands was
always blue. I've never seen them any other colour. Us kids

13

was usually pinkish but me mother's skin was sometimes a horrible colour.

The Gas Board used to dump their slag in a yard off King Street. If ye poked about, there was always cinders to be had. When I was about eleven or twelve I used to take me tatey bags down and fill them up. There was stacks of people there all doin' the same thing. Pickin' and lookin'. Your hands was often cut to ribbons but it was worth it. Ye watched for the cart comin' and marked the time. Good stuff used to drop off sometimes when they jerked along the cobbles, and if it didn't it was up to you to help it. Everybody did it. Sometimes there was nowt to be had in the yard except slag that would never burn, and ye just had no choice. I suppose it was dishonest really. But ye used to tell yerself it would have dropped off anyway and somebody else would only get it. On a good night there would be plenty, and ye'd fill yer bags and pile them against the wall while ye carried home what ye could and raced back before somebody decided to pinch it.

After a shipwreck I used to go down to the long beach at South Shields. At low tide there was driftwood and sometimes coal as well, just for the takin'. It was a long way from where we were livin' but it wasn't every day ye had a shipwreck. Me mother stopped it at the finish. The tide comes in quickly and there was so many drowned or never heard of again.

We had a canny bit of furniture by then. A rockin' chair and even a chest of drawers. We always had an iron bath in front of the fire. The youngest got washed first then the oldest. They were very particular, the older ones. They wouldn't show themselves off with nowt on, even to their own sisters. When the little ones had been bathed and gone to bed, the big'uns would get in one at a time and nobody would look. We had one tap in the yard which we shared with the neighbours.

When we had no shoes, we didn't go to school. Me mother was too proud to send us in bare feet. Then when the truant man came, me mother told him and he would give us a police ticket. This used to get ye shoes and stockin's. The shoes were heavy and black but strong, and had a stamp on that was little holes punched in in a special way, and the stockin's was black

14

with a white band. This was to make sure ye couldn't pledge them.

When I was about eight or nine, I told me mother that I wanted to have a go at sellin' the fish. I felt I had a flair for it. I knew I could do it if only I could get a start.

'No, you're far too young, pet. It's not nice for little girls to do. You stick at your schoolin' until you get a bit older.'

'Please Mam, just give's a try. I can help. I know I can.'

'No. Only I do that. None of your sisters do it.'

'But Mam, Lizzie's a fish girl.'

'Yes, I know, but not in that way. She has a proper job, packin' and cleanin' and makin' kippers and that sort of thing. Not the sellin', Francie. . . . Well, maybe just a few little fry herrin', just to try.'

Me mother used to sell around the doors carryin' the board on her head. It was made of heavy wood about three feet long, and had on it big, fat, cheap fish like blackjack and cod which she would slice up for customers just how they wanted it, with her mallet and gully. On her fingers she carried the strings of herrin'. These were the ones that had been broken by the hooks. Perfectly good fish, lovely eatin'. Just a little bit bashed up that's all. Anyway, mother used to thread the string through their gills and carry about two dozen on each line hangin' downwards. Well, a few days later, she brought me a few in a little sixpence ha'penny basket and I sold the lot; one and threepence we got for them. And so I was started.

Before I became regular at it, like doin' it properly, I was of course hawkin' the greens. And before that me main outdoor jobs had been cleanin' the maister's shoes. Captain Davidson that was. He was captain of a big ship and away most of the time. And his wife, now she was what I call a lady. I used to get one and six a week there, and that was really good money. Mind you, things had to be very clean. She was very particular. But very kind as well. Every mornin' before school, I would go round and scrub the steps and edge them white with rubbin' stone. Then I had to polish the hall all shiny, clean the kitchen and scullery, and wash the dishes. Alice, Nellie and

15

Lily had all worked there. First one and then the other. When one left they would speak for the other and they would get their place and so on. Wor Alice was in service there right up till she was married, but she got three and six for that of course.

When the maister was home from the ships, he would leave all his boots out and I would give them an extra good cleanin' and polishin'. Sometimes he left half a dollar inside his big boot. He was a good man, very kind and very generous. She was very good to me mother. She let us do her washin' and now and again she would say, 'I've got some old clothes for the children, Mrs Nichol. Send someone round for them.' Things like that.

By the time I was eleven, I would go straight from school and rent a big barrer for a shillin' in the market. I'd wheel it to the river and get the ferry across to North Shields. I could always buy the greens cheaper on that side. A far greater variety and better stuff as well, we always thought. Sometimes all the barrers would be out. Then I would just use the fish basket. That was more than three feet wide. It was round and deep. I used to have to get two fellers to lift it onter me head. It used to press down so much, I sometimes thought I would lose me neck, and I would clamp me hand tight round to stop it sinkin' in too far.

The ferry used to cost a ha'penny both ways. I'd have me barrer packed full to the brim by the time I brought it ower home. We'd empty it and I'd run back with it before I had me tea. After tea we'd sort everythin' out, clean it, pick off the bad leaves and throw them away. Folks don't like to see that sort of thing. And it spoils the look of your show. Everythin' was divided into three lots. Mornin', afternoon and night-time. Your big stuff, like rhubarb and cabbage for the dinner, was sold first thing Saturday mornin'. The radishes, scallions (spring onions) and lettuce was the afternoon load. Those was what they'd want for their tea. Then straight after tea, out with the mint, sage, wallflowers, thyme and other seasonin's. All neatly tied up in little bundles—nobody'd dream of buyin' that kind of thing before tea.

I used to try and get me tick in when I went out with the

16

small stuff. You always had the same route for greens and fish, sometimes goin' back three or four times in a day down the same backlanes where all your good customers were. Durin' the week, I would collect greens before school to sell in the afternoons, or just not go to school at all if things weren't goin' too well and try and make it up before the weekend.

Whenever me mother brought a few strings of broken herrin', I would go straight out and sell them so folks could have them for their tea, for their men comin' in. So the door sellin' changed from day to day dependin' upon whatever was due for sellin' at that time.

By the time the weekend came, I couldn't let any more tick go out. I would always have to pawn me shawl to buy me stocks with at first, and then get it back after I'd done me rounds. Poor people hadn't any money to pay ye straight away and they were always your best regular customers. Mind, the lodgin' house people had to pay cash because they were always comin' and goin'. They used to buy fish mainly, and so did the hotels like the Royal Grill, and the Criterion, although they always preferred the shell fish. We used to do them up lovely. Crabs, prawns, winkles, mussels. Boil them in the wash-tub with salt until all the white froth comes off, then scrub them pink and clean. They used to sell for maybe a penny a scoop, or twopence if they were big ones.

Of course the shell-fish, like the mint and sage, were luxuries really, and if people hadn't been able to afford to pay for their blackjack or their cabbage for instance, then ye couldn't let them have the extras as well. Not on tick that is. Especially not on a Saturday when ye had to try and get all your money in to start off the next week properly with a clean slate.

Folks were canny and I never had much trouble with anybody. I couldn't write but I could remember. 'Let's see, so and so four doors up, she owes sevenpence for cod from Tuesday.

'The fat lady in the green door, a shillin's worth of broccoli.'

I never asked for money, though. I would just shout up the stairs.

'Are you there, hinny? I've got somethin' I think you'd like. Lovely white celery down here! Crisp radishes!'

17

They would know what I meant. Sometimes the husbands would come down and say, 'How much does she owe you, pet? I'll pay you. Here!'

'Oh no, it's all right mister, not much. I'll call again later when she's in.'

Some men go mad when they find out how much the wife's run up. Other times when the women came out and seemed to forget, ye could say 'Have ye still enough onions left, or do ye need a few more?' Then they would say somethin' like, 'Oh, that reminds me, I haven't paid you for the last lot. Here you are, pet. What was it again, hinny?' And then you'd be all right.

When I got well on and had a bit of confidence, I couldn't go wrong. By then I was a big lass and very fresh coloured. Healthy as well, with long hair done up in a bun. We didn't carry a backcreel like the Cullercoats girls, but people said we were very bonny all the same. The backcreels were raffia bags with straps that they put their arm through. Everyone knew the Cullercoats girls by them. And by how pretty they were as well, so people used to say.

A clean shawl I put on every day to keep the fish scales out of me hair. They used to stink and ye got lice from the fish. If ye lost your weeze—the weeze was just a ring of straw wrapped with cloth, put in between your basket and your head—ye had to make one from your shawl and then ye had plenty of scales and lice by the time ye got back home that night. What a difference it made. Ye used to feel really proud with your shawl and fisherwoman's petticoat with folds right down to the feet, and scrubbed clogs clickin' along the cobbles. I had some lovely print aprons—not gaudy, just pretty checks. And at one time even a pair of long boots with buttonholes. Your shawl wasn't tied so tight they couldn't see your golden earrings. My, I used to really look the part. I was proper swanky in them days.

We never had proper handbrushes or toothbrushes but we did have a thin-toothed comb for the nits. We all shared that. I had never heard of talcum powder or anythin' like that, and we certainly couldn't afford what ye call make-up, but what I used to do, was to wet me finger with spittle and rub it on the

18

wallpaper. Some of the nice pink colour used to come off the roses on the design, and I used to put it on me cheeks. All us girls, if we found a little bit of old lace or some nice decoration like that, would wash it and press it, and sew it around the edges of wor dresses to make them look really posh. We had to be really sort of proper, though. Mother wouldn't have us with bare necks or anythin' indecent. No skin had to be seen, was her motto.

With hawkin', I got quite brazen and could sell anythin'. I used to shout all kinds of things. Sometimes ye got your words all mixed up. They used to run into each other and you'd forget what ye were supposed to be shoutin'. But people knew what ye meant all the same. They recognised your particular call.

'Byalabster! Byalaster! Bylaster!' That was supposed to mean, come and buy my lobster. Though we hardly ever sold those—they were too dear. We called prawns little lobsters. And if they wanted big ones, well then, they got crabs. Saturday afternoon was a good time for shellfish. After the scallion (spring onion) round and before the sage.

Me mother used to buy the fish from the quay when the herrin' season was finished. She did this in the mornin's and got loads for both of us to sell in the afternoons. If I wasn't out with the greens or if she was on the washin' then I would do it instead. The fish was auctioned very early in the mornin' as soon as the boats came in. The merchants would buy a hundred barrels or more, and then set the price. We would wait till all the dealin' was over and then buy a barrel from them. Ye could get them for threepence when there was a glut on, and sell them for fourpence or even fivepence. Good herrin' could be sold to the foreign seamen for the special meals they used to cook, and for picklin'. They bargained hard but we always got a good price by goin' around the dock places where they were. I've seen us go to North Shields four or five times back and forwards across the ferry on a good day, and get rid of it all. The fishermen were a bit rough but kind-hearted and never gave ye trouble unless ye asked for it. Me mother would never let me go on to a ship to sell. Some of the girls did and they used to stay on a long time, much longer than necessary to sell their fish. Sometimes they didn't even sell it. It put ye off seein' what happened to some of the others who would be goin' down the rope ladders with the sailors shoutin' and puttin' their hands up their skirts and everythin'. I didn't like any of that sort of thing. I went to sell fish. Mind, some of the ones ye knew would be real gentlemen. They would take ye to the Empire to see the variety show and buy ye chocolates. So they certainly weren't all bad as some'll have you believe. Not by a long chalk.

I really liked the hawkin'. Both the fish and the greens. And there were some happy times, chattin' to people who seemed to like me. I could easily sell things like the thyme and flowers which some of the girls wouldn't go near. After I'd sold mine I would take their baskets and sell theirs for them. I trained a lot of them. They would come and go but I was at it for a long time. I would show them how to watch for a good standin' pitch and then how to follow the ladies with a sprig of mint under their noses. Nobody can resist that. Arrange your flowers to look their best. Brightest ones at the front and with a couple of the best smellers in your hand to wave in the faces of the men. Especially the ones who are on their way home after a few beers.

The girls all fixed their prices. They were very fair like that, but if they got the first ferry and you missed it, some of them would go down your lanes and say ye weren't comin' today, that ye were poorly or somethin'. I still went around though for all that, and still sold me stuff even after they'd already done my lanes.

2

Wor Nellie was very sort of genteel and would rather get a situation for three and six a week than earn ten bob hawkin'. She was too polite for sellin' and was so particular that she would take off her knickers, old-fashioned ones they were, every night, and wash them ready for the next day. The rest of us would make ours last three days at a time. For all that, poor Nellie still got in the family way, with the help of Septimus Johnson. At first Sep's mother wouldn't allow them to get married. She reckoned that her son could never have done a dreadful thing like that and most certainly was not the father, although Sep himself had the decency to own up to it.

The burden of life was now beginnin' to tell on me mother. She was deeply upset enough when she found out about wor Nellie, and was shamed to distraction by what Sep's mother was goin' around sayin'.

'Tell them we'll have blood tests done, then', she said. 'It'll prove wor Sep had nowt to do wi' it. Brazen hussy that she is!'

With the others all away workin' or married, Nellie, me mother and me moved to Bird Street in North Shields, to get away from all the talk, and there me mother became very poorly.

Soon after, Sep and Nellie got married and a very weak bairn was born premature. But Sep went on livin' with his own mother until Nellie and he could get a place of their own. There was no room for him at our place, and no room for Nellie at his. Sep did not earn much as a blacksmith's apprentice so poor Nellie had to forget about tryin' to be posh, and had to take any kind of work that was goin'—in the fishhouse or anywhere else—to get enough money for me mother who was now beyond goin' to work any more. And for her own bairn. I had to stay at home to nurse both me mother and Nellie's bairn. It was so sickly that it spent all its short life wrapped in cotton wool in the fireplace. It was here and gone in a couple of months.

Even still, me mother was takin' in washin' and hand wringin' whenever she could get it.

One mornin' as Nellie was gettin' ready for work, I heard an awful noise on the landin' soundin' like a dog chokin'. I opened the door and found me mother crawlin' along the passage with a terrible look on her face.

21

'Ee Mam, what's the matter? What are you doin'?'

Nellie ran downstairs for two men who carried wor mother upstairs and gently laid her on the bed. She was quiet now and very still. The cheap doctor came later and said she had suffered a bad stroke, and told Nellie wor mother had only twenty-four hours left.

At midnight, me mother got out of bed and began pullin' down the drapes and bedhangin's. She could not speak and looked wild.

'I'm frightened,' I whispered to Nellie. 'What's happenin' to her? What can we do for her? Will she be gettin' better soon do ye think, Nellie?'

'Hush will you. I'm stayin' to watch her and you'll have to stop as well.'

Next day, me mother was a little better and we thought everythin' might be all right after all. I suppose we were too young and too daft to realise what was really happenin'.

For the next six weeks she got better and brighter every day. I used to take a jug down to the broth kitchen near Saville Street, and get free soup and a little bread bun each. This particular day I got some rice with the little money I had got from the odd washin' that I had been able to take in. The place was tidy and clean, and it smelt really lovely with the rice puddin' cookin' warmly. I opened the street door to let the sunshine in.

I pummelled the pillow and propped me mother up.

'You're gettin' champion now, Mother, aren't you?'

'Yes pet, I am. If only I get over this then I'll take in a couple of extra washings and get you a nice pair of shoes, a nice frock and a nice coat to go out in, for when you see Johnny.'

That was Johnny Robinson—the lad who was courtin' is.

'Ooh, yes, Mam. Real fancy clothes. That'll be smashin'.'

Just then the doctor came in.

'Look at that then, doctor. She's right as rain nearly, now isn't she? She's been sittin' up all by herself and chattin' away to me like a good 'un. She's goin' to be all right now, isn't she?'

'Doctor,' me mother says to him, 'I was just thinking. As it's

22

such a fine day I could mebbe go downstairs and sit at the doorstep for a little bit of fresh air. I just feel like it. It'll probably put me right, I think.'

'I don't see why not, Mrs Nichol.'

Just then, me mother gave a little gurgle and fell back on her pillow.

'She's in a faint again, doctor. She often goes into a little faint. I'll get some water.'

The doctor knocked the cup of water from me hand and on to the floor, and spilled it.

'Quickly! Put a mustard plaster on the back of her neck. Don't give her anything to drink! I'll need something from the surgery but I'll be back in a minute.'

Well, I made up the poultice quick as I could and was just gently placin' it on the back of her neck. . . .

'Oh dear, oh dear. Oh me bairn. . . ! Oh me bairn. . . ! Oh me little bairn . . .' and she sighed a long sigh.

That was the last breath the poor soul ever took. When the doctor came back they tell me I was just starin' at her canny, dead face.

'She's suddenly stopped talkin' all of a sudden, doctor!'

The doctor looked at me mother and said to somebody who was standin' there, I don't rightly remember who:

'I've seen children die like this, but never a grown-up. She was talking so lovely just then. Send that girl along to my surgery, I'll give her something. She's had an awful shock.' And he went out.

'Mam, why aren't you talkin' to me?'

And I put me hand on her heart like I'd see other people do. It was stopped. They say a big feller came in and carried me off to the doctor's in his arms. I don't remember.

By the time I was fifteen, which was 1904, all of me sisters were married. Some to good men and others to not so good. And they had all got married in the proper order, oldest first, youngest last. JaneAnne was the only one of us who never worked. Me father was still at home when she was growin' up, so she didn't have to go out to work. She wasn't much to look at and not very bright. And although she was very house-

23

proud, she hadn't much go in her. Her man, Jim Kilcaldy, had been in the navy and he was one of those hoity-toity fellers who thought he knew everythin' when in fact he knew nowt. He was a big-head but he had a good sense of humour. Always playin' jokes on somebody, he was. He was hard on wor Jenny but he was friendly enough to me. Neither of them amounted to much but at least they stuck together, I will say that.

Alice was very bright and pretty. And although we were all well built, she was the tallest. She was in service from the time she was twelve till she got married to Bob Charlton, a big handsome bloke who worked in a chemicals factory in Jarrow. He was a good worker, but a terrible lustful man. I hated him all me life for the horrible, disgustin' things he did.

Lizzie was what I would call beautiful. She was smaller than the rest of us but still very well made. And very clean. When she was about fourteen, somebody had hit her over the head with a tin can. It affected her brain for a while and all she did was sing hymns all day long. But she got better in the end and never sung no more hymns for the rest of her life.

When she was seventeen she went with two boys at the same time. One was a teetotal called John Noble and the other was wild Bob Elsdon. He could never get enough to drink. He used to come to the window at yon time of night, shoutin' about how much he loved wor Lizzie. He used to give me mother grey hairs. Lizzie used to say to her over and over again 'Mother, which one shall I take?' Me mother always replied the same 'I'm not here to choose for you. You pick your own, pet. It's you who've got to live with him.' Anyway it seems she married the wrong one, Bob Elsdon. If he was bad before he got married, he was a whole lot worse afterwards. Lizzie lost interest in herself, in keepin' the place clean. And in the bairns, all three of them. Bob died of the drink when he was little more than twenty. Lizzie wouldn't accept help and completely lost her head. They took the bairns off her and put them into a home, which was just as well because the little lad used to take these awful fits. Lizzie was sent to the workhouse where ye get your food and are kept clean, but ye have to do a bit of work if ye are able to, like makin' beds, washin' and cleanin' and that.

Anyway, she got very thick with this feller and the next thing we hear, she's out again and livin' with him. We thought this was a terrible thing and me mother once broke a cup over his head. A thing I thought I'd never see her do. Well, when me mother died, the rest of the girls and me went to seek Lizzie to tell her about the funeral. We knew she hadn't any decent clothes to wear, so we took some borrowed ones for her. But she never came.

Nellie was the brightest one of all, and the slimmest. Good lookin' as well. She was most like me mother. Always above board, never tell a lie and would hurt nobody if she could help it. She followed Lizzie into service but there was no money in it. There was in the kipper factories, though. She didn't like that sort of thing but she had to do it all the same. Splittin' the herrin's for to make kippers out of, that was their job. She gave it up of course when she met Sep. He was a man worth havin'. He was good to wor Nellie, and good to me as well.

Lily was clever and rather nice lookin'. She wasn't anythin' startlin' mind you, but more than just passable. She'd went straight into the herrin' business as soon as she was old enough. She married a feller called Jack Bee. They both worked hard on shift work at the Fish House in Shields. From six o'clock at night till six o'clock in the mornin'. Although Jack was a generous chap he also drank a lot. But I think wor Lily deserved him because she liked her drink as well. Too much I think. I used to mind her bairns when she was out workin', but then she was havin' them so quick she could hardly work at all. First one then another, and so it went on. I was workin' very hard meself, hawkin', besides lookin' after her bairns, and she wasn't very kind to is.

3

Me father had called a few times to see me mother when she was very ill, near the last, and me mother had often spoke of havin' him back and givin' him another chance. Some people

25

said he was a rotten waster, but when ye saw your own father on the corner of the street just standin' there and lookin' at you, ye couldn't just pass him by. I loved me mother and didn't have much time for what he'd done to her, but he was still me father when all was said and done.

Ye'd see him leanin' against a wall and not lookin' very well with nothin' in his pocket for a drink, and ye couldn't help wantin' to give him somethin' just to get a glass of beer with. Ye didn't know if he had anywhere to stay or anythin' to eat. He used to do little bits of jobs here and there when he could get it. Mebbe doin' a bit of bricklayin' or choppin' a few sticks. He always had his hodman's cap on, but ye could still see he was goin' white here and there. Me mother always thought of him and when she knew where he was stayin', she would send little bits of things for him when she could. Mebbe a bit of pie or do a bit of cleanin' up for him so that he'd be comfortable.

When I was about seven or eight, she once sent me round to his place. We hadn't seen him for quite a while before that and she was worried. So when she heard where he was, she told me to wait until he'd gone out and then go in and get everythin' spick and span for him comin' back. He had this room in Thames Street. I took round a pail and some cleanin' stuff and waited till he'd gone out. Then I went in and cleaned everythin' from top to bottom. Me mother said I had to have everythin' sparklin' white, and so I put whitenin' in the bucket and did the whole lot. Stairs, table, chairs, pepper-pot, anythin' and everythin' I could lay me hands on. Oh it was beautiful and white when I'd finished. You've never seen anythin' like it. When I'd finished, I brought in old Mrs Easton from next door.

'Look Mrs Easton, I've got me da's house all lovely and bonny. Come and see it and see what I've done.'

When Mrs Easton saw it she said, 'Oh my godfather!' and I thought she seemed pleased. Anyway, the top and bottom of it was, that she took me back to me mother and then sent me for a message. While I was away she told me mother what I'd done, and she sent two of the other girls round as soon as they came in to try and get rid of all the white. Me father heard

26

about it and told me mother never ever to send me anywhere near his house again.

JaneAnne and Jim took him in for a while and that was a satisfactory arrangement as far as me mother was concerned. She knew he was being looked after when he was there, and that Jim wouldn't let him mess around too much if he could help it, because Jim loved me mother like a son would.

Me mother never asked me father for anythin' except once, when we were really scrapin' the barrel in North Shields and me mother was ill. She told him she wanted nothin' for herself, or the other girls who could fend for themselves, as long as he'd give her a few shillin's a week for me. She was goin' to take him to court but he said he could only earn a few bob for himself as he was nearly always out of work. They could never find out exactly how much he was gettin' anyway because he was always subbin' his wages for beer money. So me mother never again bothered after that. If he didn't really want to give it to her, well, that was that. There was no way of makin' him.

He hadn't helped to bury me mother of course. The rest of us had been puttin' so much aside for her when she was ill just in case there was a funeral, but that had vanished. We used to have an insurance man come for the twopence a week and me mother used to leave it on the mantelpiece for him when we were out. But after she died we found he'd never been puttin' it down in his book and we never saw him again. I had asked me father to go into debt to give her a decent funeral but he wouldn't. Me sisters and brothers that was married had to instead.

A few days before me mother died, we were chattin' away. I think now that she must have known she was goin' to die soon, because she says to me: 'You know, Francie, when I get over this, I think I'll give your dad another chance. He might mend his ways now that he is gettin' older. And it means that when I go, he can look after you and you can look after him. Just the two of you together. It'll be a start for you for when you get married.'

So after she went I decided I'd do what me poor mother would have wanted me to do. And I really thought in me own

27

heart he deserved another chance. So a few weeks later, I came back to South Shields, found a little room in Foster Street, and brought him in. I was nearly fifteen then.

I said, 'Look Dad, let's pull together and make a real happy home of it. I've started with the greens again and make a canny few coppers out of that, and you must be gettin' a few bob from your odd jobs. We can pay the rent easy. . . . It's only two bob a week. We can get a few sticks of furniture and some food and I'll make some nice meals for we to eat, and I'll keep the place spankin' clean. And we can mebbes put a little bit away for a rainy day.'

I didn't think I was askin' too much of him now and I knew he was in better straits. When the weather was fine he could usually find some kind of work. Anyway, he agreed to me plan and we got started. I didn't like that place in Foster Street very much. We'd always had some beetles and mice wherever we'd been. You've got to expect that. But there it was wick with them and I'm not over fond of beetles. But at least it was a little home, beetles or no beetles. And it only cost us one and six a week rent.

A gill of beer, and half an ounce of baccy, had to be laid on for him every day. He was always comin' in drunk at yon time of night and I was out all day with the greens. I used to do the housework before I went to work and then come back in time to have his dinner ready in case he came back for it. Whenever I had a lot of tick goin' I was havin' to pawn me skirt and shoes at night to get startin' money for the next day. One day I made up me mind I'd had enough so I made him a lovely meal to get him into a good mood. Sausages fried, black puddin' and potatoes, and an extra bottle of beer with his baccy.

'I'm goin' out with the prawns now, Dad, and I'll need some money to get the shoppin' in. Can you give is a few shillin's?'

When I came home he asked for it back. I told him I'd spent it, and that instead of him keepin' me, I was keepin' him. He went mad! He bashed is from one end of the room to the other and though I was strong and sturdy, I couldn't defend meself against him. He gave me one hell of a hidin' that night. Fortunately for me, the neighbours heard the screams and the

28

shoutin' and they dragged him off and threw him out.

'Get the rentbook and keep it, Francie. Hide it pet. Don't let him get his hands on it, then the police can't put you out.'

So I did as I was bid and locked all the doors. I could still hear him shoutin', 'I'll come back and murder ye when I get in, ye little bitch!'

I never slept a wink all that night. In the mornin' the neighbours came again and asked is if I'd had any breakfast.

'No. I won't dare gan out in case he gets in and kills is. I know he's hidin' in the coalhouse waitin' his chance.'

'We'll have a look for ye, pet, and tell ye if it's safe. No, he's not here! It's alreet, ye can come oot, Francie.'

'Ye'll have to fetch our JaneAnne and her man with ye before I open this door.'

Half an hour later Jim and JaneAnne came in with me father and told him he had to pack up and go away with them. He got his gear and left without a word.

I wasn't goin' to stay there by meself with all them beetles, so I told me sisters they could have whatever they wanted from the house. I wanted nothin' but to get out of it.

JaneAnne said I had to go and live with her until I got somewhere to go. I stayed with them for about six months before I left in the finish because I couldn't stand her spiteful, silly ways. They were both as mean as sin. They took every penny I was gettin' and I had to watch him and me father drinkin' it all away. So I left and went to live with me other sister, Alice, who was livin' in Jarrow.

Wor Alice, I'm sorry to say, turned out to be every bit as mean as wor JaneAnne, and much less considerate. Not only did she want everythin' I earned, but she pawned the only dress I had so that I couldn't go out at night. They didn't care how I earned me keep as long as I handed over every penny. The few shillin's I got from pullin' potatoes was no gift by any stretch of the imagination. Gilroy's tatey fields were well known for their cheap and hard labour. I'd had to give up the greens and the fish. They take a lot of cleanin' and preparin' before ye can set them out on your tray. And that takes time as well if you're to do the job properly. And with me mother gone

I had nobody at home to help is. Anyway, Alice wouldn't have the fish and all the mess that goes with it at her house. So I just had to do the tatey work instead. She would always keep is hungry. I was growin' and I was strong and I had an appetite like a man. Funny thing was in them days, the men always had twice as much to eat as the women. It didn't matter how big or small you were.

At dawn I would be up and dressed and out, waitin' with the other people for the carts to come and take us to the fields. Dressed, that is, in clothes fit only for grubbin' round in soil and clay all day. None of your lace shawls or cotton frocks for that job. We wore tough sackcloth that would still keep together long after ye'd lost your fingernails among the tateys. Ye could rely on your bare feet, but not on cheap clogs. Along with all the other poor tatey pickers, I would be carted back when it became too dark to pull any more of their precious spuds. Then we all hurried home from the place where they dumped we off, hopin' in our heart of hearts we wouldn't meet anybody special before we got back and got wor raggy claes (clothes) off. There was no time and no point in dreamin' about bein' a lady in those days. It was a luxury just to get washed and get to bed.

It was about this time that I nearly did somethin' which I've always been deeply ashamed of and I'll never forgive meself to the day I die for ever lettin' such a thought ever enter me head. I was so hungry this day, I didn't know what to with meself, nor what I was doin'. Ye were starvin' after a day in the tatey fields, and when ye knew the chance was there'd be next to nowt on the table when ye got back, I don't know, it made ye worse than the lowest animal. Even dogs can scratch around bins and nobody says nowt. And they used to say if Gilroy's caught ye pinchin' a tatey ye got put in jail. Well, this day, I went up to a big house in this strange lane intendin' to ask for a slice of bread to eat. Just as I knocked on the door, a great big dog started barkin' in the yard and I ran off. And by God I'm glad I did, 'cos that big dog saved my soul that day, and me peace of mind ever since.

Shortly after that, I went to Hood Haggies Ropery to seek a

job. I knew the work would be rough, but it was regular, and I needed a change from Gilroy's. Me hands had become hard as cobs. They were calloused, and had black dirt ingrained in the cracks. Just like an old miner's.

Mr Blyth was stout and he was strict. Seemin'ly very hard on the outside, but really quite soft on the inside when ye got to know him. He was a good man to me.

'How old are you, lassie?'

'Fifteen.'

'You're too young.'

'But I've got to have work.'

'You're far too young. You should still be at school. Come back when you're sixteen. Next one!'

I went back the next day hopin' to see a different gaffer, and stood in the queue. I had put me hair up in a bun and tried to put a frown on me face to make is look older.

'How old are you?'

'Sixteen.'

'Name? Hey! Wait a minute. . . . Weren't you here the other day? Yes, I've seen you before. Now when was it?'

'Yesterday.'

'That's right. I told you you were too young, didn't I?'

'Yes, I know, but I'm sixteen today.'

'I thought as much.'

'Look, Mister, if ye would only give is a chance, I'll do anythin'. I'll make a good job of it. I can scrub and clean and do all sort of things. I've put. . . .'

'All right. All right. You certainly seem game enough. I'll start you and see how you get on. If you're no good by the end of the week, then you're out on your ear. Fair enough?'

'Right Mister! Thanks. That's fair enough by me. Thank you kindly.'

I was given the job of puttin' the raw fibre stuff in the drums, on a conveyor belt. As the drum moved along ye had to knee them into place, and after two or three days of this, me legs was badly bruised and swollen, and me hands raw from the sharp fibres. However, I dare not let on in case Mr Blyth thought I was too soft for the job.

Two weeks later Mr Blyth seemed quite satisfied with is and said I was bein' put on the machines. It was a kind of promotion with plenty responsibility, and it was more interestin'. And it put a couple of bob more in me pay packet. But it turned out such a fiddle with those damn' machines, I didn't know what to pull and what to push. Whether ye had to screw this knob in or that one out, which lever ye had to twist up and which one ye had to twist down. Well, I got meself into an awful knot and this big handle came down and split me hand. There was blood everywhere. I was scared stiff I'd get the sack, so I bound me hand round with some rope strands to make a bandage, and mopped up the blood with some more, and chucked it away out of sight. This canny feller came over and put the machine right for is and showed is what to do. When Mr Blyth heard about it and he came over, and though I tried me bestest to keep it hidden, he saw me hand. I told him it was nothin'. It had only got scratched a bit and looked far worse than it was. He said I had to go to the First Aid place. When I came back, he put is on a different job. Any road, he said as I was a good worker, and such a relief from some of the hard cases he had to deal with, he would still keep is on. Me new job was to watch for knots comin' down the line and lift the rollers to free them, and then chuck the stuff into these big cans. There was a shillin' bonus to be had on this machine if ye could work it fast enough, but I could never win it. It was all I could do to keep it runnin' at all, let alone get it to gan faster.

One day Mr Blyth comes up and says:

'I don't know what's the matter with you, Nichol. You're too slow to catch cold. Goodness only knows how you were brought up or what kind of parents you've got, but you certainly. . . .'

'Don't you dare talk about my parents, Mister! I haven't got any. So don't ever say anythin' about them. I'm tellin' you straight!'

He just ups and away without another word and I thought I'd had me chips. Anyway I carried on, and an hour after, he came back and said he was very sorry, and that he'd only been tryin' to spur is on because he knew I needed the bonus. He shifted is yet again to another job but this time I could easily make the grade. It's just as well an' all because if he'd moved is anywhere else I'd have been put ootside altogether. I was always on to the poor feller for ways to make a little bit more than I was gettin'.

'Is there any chance of overtime for me this week, Mr Blyth?'

'How should I know? You'll just have to look on the board like anybody else and see if your name's chalked up.'

But it always was, canny man, it always was.

There was some very tough people worked in the ropery and if the rest of them thought somebody had been showed any favours, their life wouldn't be worth livin'. They could do some awful things to ye. Awful . . . I wouldn't mind to speak about the things a gang of women can do when there's no men about. It was their kind of justice though, ye see, and ye could understand it if ye were brought up with it. These were rough people but poor people. They each thought they were just as good as the next and that nobody deserved any more than anybody else—of good luck or bad. And there was one thing they never had no doubts about. If they didn't take care of theirselves, nobody else would. Because nobody cared. Ye can't really blame them for cursin' and swearin', can ye? That's the way they were and they knew no different ways. They used to pass their dinner time kickin' an old tin can around because they had nothin' else to do. Ye don't wear ballgowns and top hats when ye spend yer days in a dirty black factory.

They were a canny lot, men and women alike. I remember once gettin' me shawl caught in a machine. I used to wear it to try and keep some of the dirt out of me hair, and also to stop me hair gettin' caught in the machine and endin' up as rope. Somebody had bumped against is, and me head went back into the machine. It dragged me shawl around me neck so that I was gettin' strangulated and I couldn't shout out because me throat was choked. It all happened so quickly. Well, this oiler feller who was workin' up above, saw what was goin' on, and quick as a flash he jumped straight down and stopped the machine and cut the shawl off me neck with a knife.

33

c

Meanwhile, at home, although I could put up with me sister's meanness, me brother-in-law, Bob Charlton, was causin' is a lot of embarrassment. Everybody except wor Alice, his own wife, knew how randy he was. I used to wake up in the middle of the night and see this big feller standin' at the bottom of me bed graspin' the rail and starin' at is with a horrible look in his eyes. At last I couldn't stand it any longer and was afraid in case Alice should find out and think I was leadin' him on. Luckily Nellie and Sep knew what he was like and took me in with them. They were very kind to me. Nellie treated me like a daughter, and Sep, like as if I was his young sister. They made me give up the ropeworks and I went into service for four months at a house in Wallsend.

Not that I was much better off. The lady of the house was a proper bitch and kept her husband and me right under her thumb. I lived in with them and worked until one o'clock in the mornin' every day, for three shillin's a week, with the odd half day off. Several times I dropped down in a dead faint through sheer hard work and lack of sleep. The old man was kind to me when he dared, and I appreciated it. One mornin' he had tangled up the venetian blinds in tryin' to get them open, and he was so terrified out of his mind, that I said I'd take the blame. The old woman, she wasn't really old, got herself in a terrible rage and grabbed hold of me neck, and holdin' a pair of scissors in her hand, said she would cut me fingers off if such a thing ever happened again. I had to put up with every kind of insult rather than go back to be a burden on our Nellie, but the time came when I could take no more. I gave a month's notice to the Mistress as she called hersel', but she wouldn't take it.

'You shall have no money and none of your belongings until you promise me you will do no such thing, you cheeky, worthless little upstart!'

Nevertheless, on me next afternoon off, I put on as many clothes as I could without 'rousing her suspicions, and I left. Nellie took is back and told is that she would go and see the lady. Poor meek and mild Nellie was no match for that tartar though, and both me wages that was owin', and me few little bits and pieces and mementoes of me mother, she kept for herself. And I never saw her or me belongin's ever no more.

4

I first met Johnny Robinson when we were kids playin' in the street. We were both about twelve or thirteen at the time. The boys would run off with wor hats and when we came after them, the boys would turn around, take hold of us, and give us a kiss.

They used to say the Robinsons owned half of South Shields. Streets of houses, and some very large lodgin' houses. They were hard and they were tough and boxin' was in their blood. In those days, the name Robinson meant boxin' and property. Johnny's father, Henry Robinson, had been a fighter. His Uncle Johnny had been a champion barefist fighter in the eighties. And his father before him. But young Johnny, when I first met him, was very quiet and shy. They said he should have been a Catholic priest. He was thin but very healthy lookin'. Tall and dark-haired and good to look at with his grey eyes and fresh colourin'. Before I met him, I knocked about with a Protestant lad called Dick Jennin's. But one day, Johnny Robinson said to is 'I'm taking you off him.' I was Johnny's girl from then on. For two years that was the way it was and it suited me, because I had always fancied Johnny, although I never thought anythin' could come of it. What with me being a poor Protestant and him bein' a Catholic from a rich and respected family.

We were carryin' on together one night when I asked him for a pin. He took one from his lapel and dropped it on the ground. Then he stepped on it and grinded it with his boot.

'What did ye do that for, Johnny?'

'Because you're not even worth that pin.'

'Oh well, if that's the way ye feel, all right. That's it then isn't it.'

35

I just walked away and that was the end of that. Why? For what reason? I didn't know and I certainly wasn't goin' to get down on bended knee to ask for explanations. If that was the way he wanted it, then that was good enough for me. It eventually turned out, that Johnny had heard about wor Nellie havin' gotten in the family way and Mrs Robinson had told him that what one sister will do, another will do.

Well, long after this had happened, it must have been 1909, when I was about nineteen, I was standin' outside the *Gazette* office in South Shields. Nellie and Sep had moved to South Shields and I was now lookin' for a job nearby to try to keep down the expense of travellin'.

Suddenly, a voice spoke up, 'Isn't that you, Francie?' I turned round to face Johnny's brother Harry. 'How are you keeping? You must come and see me mother. When did you come back to Shields?'

Bein' as I was always clean and a hard worker, I think Mr and Mrs Robinson had always been quite taken with is. When I was hawkin' I used to go 'round with me fish and greens down their streets, and sellin' me shellfish to their lodgers. While I had been goin' with their Johnny, they had told is to call at their lodgin' houses. They said it would be good business for me. It had been as well.

'No, Harry, I can't. I'd like to see your mother and father, but I can't. Your brother might be there. He'll only think. . . .'

'Who? Our Johnny, you mean? Don't be silly. That doesn't matter. Anyway he'll be at work. He's servin' his time at the shipyard as a plater and riveter. It's only three o'clock. You'll be gone long before he gets back.'

'All right then, Harry. Just for a little while, to be sociable.'

'Well, well, if it isn't little Francie? And not too little at that now, I must say. Getting to be a big girl now, eh Henry?'

'A big girl; a fine big lass.'

'Now, tell me what has been happening to you and your family. Have some tea, Francie, to warm you up.'

'Oh, no thanks, Mrs Robinson. I have to be gettin' back, me sister will be worried, and I said I wouldn't be long.'

36

'Rubbish, there's plenty time. You tell her you've been to Mrs Robinson's house. That will set everything all right. Now don't you worry, do you hear? Now there's some tea.'

Mrs Robinson poured a little bit of the tea from her own mug into a saucer for me to drink.

'Now drink that. It will do you the world of good. Keep you on your mettle and keep you going till you get back home for your meal.'

Anybody lucky enough to be invited to drink tea with Mrs Robinson, always got it just like that. On a saucer poured straight from her own mug. And if you didn't like it like that, you could bloody-well lump it. Nobody stood up to Sarah Robinson, except Mr Robinson. And nobody ever backchatted him. He was a quiet man and didn't like any fuss. But he was very, very strong and couldn't be bothered with small matters. If he got out of his chair to settle an argument, somebody went to the floorboards before he sat down again. And that would have meant Mrs Robinson as well if she gave him cause enough.

'Thank you, Mrs Robinson, but I must go straight after this.'

Suddenly the door opened and Johnny Robinson was standin' there lookin' at me. He was a lot darker now, especially around the eyes, and had his hair cropped short at the sides. He wasn't smilin' or anythin'. Just lookin' straight at me. He took his jacket off and started washin' heself at the sink. Mr Robinson had gone out and Mrs Robinson was still talkin'. Nobody else had noticed Johnny come in. His muffler was tossed to the floor and he was flushin' his face at a runnin' tap. I could see his muscles goin' up and down his arms as he was flingin' the cold water over heself. His vest was drippin' wet but he still didn't take it off. He couldn't have cared less about me. I could see that. I made up me mind to go there and then.

'Ta ta then, Mrs Robinson, I really must go now. I've stayed too long as it is.' I got up and left quickly. It was easy to take your leave of the Robinsons. They wouldn't waste time settin' you to the door. You just got up and got out.

37

I had no fare and a long way to walk home. Nellie only allowed is to stay out one night a week and then only until seven o'clock. I was hurryin' up Mill Hill and it was quite dark. All of a sudden I heard these long stridin' footsteps behind is.

'That you, Francie? It's me, Johnny.'

We walked over the hill together without speakin' a word.

'I'd set you home, Francie, but it'll have to be by the backways.'

'If I'm not good enough for you to set me frontways, Johnny Robinson, then none at all.'

But I knew in me mind that I still loved him so much he could have set is home anyways he pleased.

'I'm matched to fight, Francie, and I can't be seen with a woman. That's the way it has to be with boxers. My father would go mad if anybody saw us.'

'Well, all right if that's the case.'

When we got to Nellie's house, I told Johnny that he couldn't come in.

'Wor Nellie'll play war, Johnny. I'm long past my time, any road. And she's very particular.'

We sat down on the doorstep for a while.

'When can I see you again, Francie?'

'It's up to you.'

'Right, what about next week. Next Saturday eh?'

'I suppose that might be all right, I think. I don't think I've got anything special on that night. When ye come, just knock on the door or give a whistle. I'll know it's you.'

'I can't whistle very loud.'

'Well then, just knock on the door. Everythin's quite above board here ye know, Johnny Robinson. And anybody who's clean is welcome in.'

'Goodnight then, Francie.'

'Goodnight, Johnny.'

When I got in, Nellie told is off for bein' out so late and for keepin' strange boys talkin' outside at that time of night. It was nearly seven o'clock.

'Yes, but it was Johnny Robinson, and I've got an offer of a

38

job at his brother Harry's house.' Mind, I didn't dare to tell her it was a common lodgin' house. I knew full well that she would never allow is inside one of those places.

'All right then, Francie, we'll see. Next time, bring the young man in and let's have a look at him.'

She'd forgotten about Johnny after all these years. He was a man now. She'd get a shock when she saw how he'd growed up. Tall and handsome and strong he was.

Well, when he did come, Nellie took to him straight away and made him very welcome. Everythin' went along well and I started muckin' out Harry's lodgin' house in Barrington Street, next to the Trustee's Bank. It was quite near Mill Street where the Robinsons lived.

After a couple of months or more, Johnny asked if I would mind waitin' a while before gettin' married.

'How long do ye mean?'

'I don't know. But it will be quite a long time yet, because of the boxing. So would you wait, Francie?'

'No, I certainly would not. I'm not waitin' donkey's years for you or anybody else for that matter. D'ye think I'm soft in the head or somethin'? No, if somebody comes along who's just as good as you, and if I like him as much as I like you, then I'll marry him instead.'

Shortly afterwards I found I was in the family way. Nellie had many a time told is that if I ever got meself into any kind of trouble, she would have to put is out. They hadn't enough money and they couldn't be lookin' after a whole lot of illegitimate kids.

'I'm warning you, Francie,' she used to say, 'any of you-know-what kind of monkey business, and we'll have to send you to the workhouse. Mark my words.'

Now that it had actually happened in truth, I didn't know which way to turn. Me pride wouldn't allow is to tell Johnny after what he had said the last time I saw him, and I dare not tell Nellie out of fear for what she would do. I thought probably our JaneAnne would understand best. She was the oldest and had seen quite a lot one way or another.

JaneAnne gave is her solemn word that she would never

39

breathe a word to anybody, and above all, not to our Nellie.

'Get some Epsom salts and drink a large glassful while you're sitting in as hot a tub of water as you can bear, and see if that does the trick,' was her advice.

Me mind was much eased, so I thanked her again for her help and good advice, and particularly for promisin' to definitely keep it a secret. By this time, Sep was out of his time and earnin' good money as a blacksmith and he and Nellie were the best off of all of we.

Nellie used to take a little hamper of food to the other sisters whenever she could, and the night followin' my visit, happened to be JaneAnne's turn. JaneAnne was so grateful that she blabbed out the situation I was in.

When Nellie came back I was tucked up in me bed.

'You're abed a lot sooner than usual, Francie. What's the matter with you?'

'I've got a bad cold, Nellie, and I'm tryin' to sweat it out of me system. I've just had a hot bath.'

'I know what's wrong with you, Francie Nichol. And you won't sleep that one off, my girl. You'd better do something about it. You'll have to tell him yourself. And the sooner the better.'

Two days later, Johnny called to take is out. I told him everythin'.

'That's all right, Francie, I don't think any the worse of you. But I can't marry you, you know that. And anyway I've fallen in with this other girl.'

'Well, that's all right, Johnny, I'm not complainin'. I didn't expect you to marry me anyway. I don't really want to marry you either if you really want to know. I was just tellin' you that's all. Tata then, Johnny, I have to go home, I've got a toothache. I'll just get the tram meself.'

Pretendin' the toothache, I sobbed me heart out all the way back in me handkerchief so nobody'd know what I was really doin'.

Several weeks went by and I never saw hide nor hair of Johnny. Meanwhile, he had told his brother, Harry who in turn had told Mrs Robinson. Harry couldn't even keep his own water, let alone somebody else's secret. Mrs Robinson presently sent for me to come to her house and do some cleanin' for her, and I didn't dare refuse. As I was scrubbin' the stairs, one of the boards came away and I found a calico bag full of gold sovereigns. I was flabbergasted. I'd never seen so much money in all me born days. Mrs Robinson suddenly came up behind is.

'Just roll it up and put it back where you found it, Francie. There's a good girl.'

I did as I was bid and said nowt.

Three or four of the rooms had been made into one big one, and everythin' took place there. Business deals, contractin' of marriages, eatin', smokin', drinkin', entertainin', sparrin', the lot. The furniture was massive. High sideboards and heavy wooden chairs. Great, big, long sofas and deep armchairs. The fireplace looked like the barracks armoury with all the huge iron tongs and pokers and things.

As I went round polishin' and cleanin', I knew that Mrs Robinson was never very far away.

'Francie! Anything wrong with you?'

'I don't know what you mean, Mrs Robinson. I'm quite all right.'

'You're having a baby, aren't you. Who's the father?'

'That I can't tell you, Mrs Robinson. I wouldn't tell nobody that.'

Just at that, Johnny came in.

'Mother, I'm the father of it. I'm the father', he said again, bold as brass.

'Oh, are you now? Fetch your father!'

'Well,' said Mr Robinson. 'Fine mess this is isn't it?'

'I know it is, Mr Robinson, and I am very ashamed of myself.'

'It's not you, Francie. It's him. And I'm tellin' you this, he'll never work to keep you. Did you think he would?'

'Well then, Mr Robinson, I can tell you this. If he's sick, I'll work to keep him. If he's not, he'll have to work or get out.'

'You know you'll have to become a Catholic, Francie?'

41

'I realise that, Mr Robinson, and I have no objections there.'

'You'll have to go and see the priest a few times before you get married.'

'You'd better ask him if he wants is, first.'

'I don't want anybody else, Dad. She was my first girl.'

'Right! That's that! There's nobody I'd rather him have, Francie. Don't worry. I'll see to everything. Food, wedding and all that. Leave it to me. You just carry on with what you're doing.'

5

Mr Robinson was as good as his word. He got us a little two-roomed flat in Mill Street and put in sufficient furniture to make it quite comfortable. Not new, but good secondhand stuff. We were married at St Bede's Church on the 9 October 1909.

The weddin' lasted for a week. The reception was at the Robinsons' place. There were three pianos in the big room and most of the time they were all goin' at the same time. I've never seen so much drink in all me life. The more they drunk, the more there was to be drunk. Somebody was always rollin' these great big barrels of beer in. When the Robinsons drank they drank. No taps or glasses. Just off with the lid and in with your mug. Scoop it out and get it down you. Mind ye they had plenty of food as well. Set out like a pub buffet, with massive bowls of steamin' hot tateys, steaks, bread, cheese. And broth with everythin' in it. They just stuck it all over the table and ye had to help yersel' or ye got nowt. They were a very rough lot but you never heard them blasphemin'—they were good Catholics. The whole lot of them loved music. That, fightin', and drinkin' was really all they ever cared about. Fiddlers were hired and when they had had enough they brought fresh ones in. Irish jig fiddlers were only too willin' to play till they dropped for a few shillin's and as much whiskey as they could get their hands on.

Mrs Robinson was as mean as sin with everybody. With her family, her tenants and lodgers alike. But when it came to the drink, she was generous to a fault. The sons, Geordie and Harry, were there, and the daughters, Lily with her man Stoker, and young Mary Ellen. Stoker thought too much about his boxin' to drink himself sick, but not his wife nor Geordie, nor Harry who all loved it so much you'd think God had created them for no other reason than to just drink beer.

My Johnny had a sweet voice and Lily's was like a nightingale's. Mrs Robinson would get them goin' and keep them goin'. Mr Robinson, the great big man, sat in his big chair smokin' his pipe and takin' it all in, smilin' to heself. He would be swiggin' from this huge mug, far bigger than anybody else's, and sayin' not a word. But watchin' everybody like a hawk. Many's the time I've seen him sittin' in that chair lookin' and waitin' when there was trouble brewin', then all of a sudden jump up and lay somebody out, and then sit right down again without sayin' a word.

Mrs Robinson was just the opposite. She couldn't keep her mouth shut and ye'd hear her shoutin', 'Gis a song, wor Lily! Howay woman! It gans like this . . . "I know a lass. . . ." Hey you're not singin', wor Geordie. C'mon lad, sing up so we can all hear ye. She's not dancin'! What the hell's the matter with you, Mary? Give that stupid bugger a clip on the ear. E's nearly asleep. Kick his arse for him!'

Then she'd stand up straight as a plank with her back to the fireplace.

'I'll take anybody on! C'mon you spunkless gets. Are you frightened of a woman? If I was a man, I'd be champion of the world. C'mon you, d'ye want a fight? Howay, put them up. Have you got no fire in yer belly, ye useless nowt? Will nobody make a match? Here's wor Geordie! He'll have a go. Howay then, try and hit me, you stupid bugger. Hit your own mother, would you? Well take that you impudent little sod. There's a pretty spot in Ireland I'll always claim for my land. . . .'

'Sing! Sing! Everybody sing! Top up you. Sing!'

43

The accordion feller had his backside kicked for askin' for a pound. He was certainly worth it, but he didn't get it. The priest didn't call that week, I'm sure of it.

Before the week was half done, Johnny and me left. We hadn't a honeymoon or anythin' like that. We just went. It was mainly my doin' I suppose. I got sick of it all. I wasn't used to it and I wanted to get Johnny away.

By this time, Johnny had made his mark with the boxin'. When he was only ninteeen he had won the Thompson Knockout Cup competition, and although it mightn't always show, boxin' was in his blood. He used to hang round for his father to set him up against whoever he could get to meet him. Whoever Mr Robinson got, Johnny fought. I used to tell him it was no life for us. I wanted him to finish his time as a riveter at the shipyards. But all he thought about was boxin', boxin', boxin'. His pal, Matty Cocklin, had gone to the South Bank at Middlesbrough, with the other apprentices. There was more work there.

'Why don't we go, Johnny? Finish your time and make somethin' of yourself.'

'Oh shut up, Francie. You talk too much.'

'It's only for your own good. I don't want to see ye lookin' all bashed up.'

'Shut up, I said.'

'But Johnny, there's a bairn comin' on.'

'Anyway, I've got no money for the fare to go to Middlesbrough.'

'Well, ask your mother. She's got plenty. She'll give it to ye.'

But Mrs Robinson said no, and Johnny daresn't ask his father.

'All right, Johnny, we'll still go. I'll pawn your jacket and waistcoat.'

At last, he agreed for my sake.

Johnny went next day and I followed after arrangin' for the removal of the furniture and stuff.

Mrs Robinson came to visit us and everythin' was hunky-dory. I was by now very heavy, and Johnny was very kind and considerate. He washed dishes and even helped with the sewin' and so on. Holdin' the hanks for is and that. We had a little room of our own, and Johnny wasn't drinkin' much. He would go out at night to play cards with Matty and his pals at the watchman's hut. A few games of billiards, a few beers, but never too many. I was very, very happy durin' those few weeks.

One mornin' a letter came from Mr Robinson, tellin' Johnny to come at once to talk over some very important business.

'I'll have to go right away to see what me father wants, Francie.'

'When will ye be back then, Johnny, so I'll know when to put your bait up for work?'

'Well, let's see. It's Friday today. I'll go tonight and I'll be back by Sunday, probably.'

'Sunday night you mean? You'll be back on Sunday night will ye Johnny? I'll put somethin' nice up for ye ready for goin' to work on Monday mornin'.'

Johnny left that night.

Two weeks went by without a word, and no money. My time was drawin' near and I got worried about Johnny. A kind old lady up the street had been like a mother to me and even though I hated takin' me problems to anybody else I was so desperate I went and asked the old woman what I should do.

'Write to him, pet. Tell him you've got no money and the bairn could be born any day now. Tell him, he'll have to come back and tell you what's happening or what's wrong if anything is wrong. I'm sure everything'll be all right. You know what men are. He hasn't seen his people for a while and they're probably having a bit of a get-together. Maybe he's got the 'flu or something and he's waiting till he gets better before travelling back. His mother's probably made him stay in bed for a couple of days. It's very cold out just now you know.'

'No, it's not that, missus. It can't be that. Johnny's never ailed a thing in his life. Nothin' ever bothers him. I've never known a fitter man in me life. He's always glowin' with health.'

'Well, you just sit yourself down here at this table. Here's a

45

pen, and I'll get you some paper. Go on now, Francie, write straight away. I'll go and put the kettle on and make a nice cup of tea.'

But another week passed by and still I had no word from Johnny.

I sold the flour and bread I had stowed away in the cupboard to get money for the fare back to Shields, and off I went after askin' the old lady to keep an eye on things till I got back.

When I arrived at the Robinsons they were all sittin' round in the big room. Mr Robinson spoke first and said Johnny was startin' to box, but this time it was to be all out. He was goin' professional and had to give up his job in the shipyards for keeps.

'You don't mean it, Johnny? You're not goin' to give everythin' up and stay here are ye? What about the bairn and me? Boxin'll do you no good. Look what happened to your Uncle Johnny.'

'Hold your tongue, woman! I've told you not to talk about him. You don't know anything!'

'But we were just beginnin' to do all right. We were gettin' on very canny down in Middlesbrough and you've got some canny pals there. Matty's doin' well. All our things are there now. Our home, and everythin'.'

'My father wants me to do it, and I'm going to do what he wants. He knows best. He's matched me to fight next week. And that's that.'

'But what'll I do? I've got no money.'

'Pack the stuff up, whatever you want, and get back here as soon as you can.'

'But how are we goin' to live when I do?'

'My father says he'll put you in one of the lodging houses so you can be here and earn your keep.'

'What, live in a common lodgin' house? With all those low men and all that. And I've no money to quit the landlord.'

'There's as good as you stays there, so just get on with it. You'll have to manage the best you can.'

So I went back to Middlesbrough. When I got there, I had

46

no money for food, no money to move the furniture, no money for me own fare back, or for anythin' else.

Then Lizzie arrived. She had got fed up with Geordie's antics and had made up her mind to come and stay with me instead. It was a Godsend as it turned out.

'Them bloody Robinsons! I like to see a good mill as much as anybody, but fightin' comes between them and their wits. And that old bitch. . . . I know what I'd like to do to her. They're all the same.'

'My Johnny's not.'

'Your Johnny!'

'I want to get back to him as soon as I can. That's all I care about. I married him, not them.'

'I'll go back with you if you pay me fare, Francie.'

'Lizzie, I haven't got two ha'pennies to rub against each other, and I mean it, not one even.'

'I'll tell you what. Get the money to go into Middlesbrough town and I'll get enough when we get there.'

'How'll I get it?'

'Borrow it. You must know somebody who'll lend you it.'

'I mean how'll you. . . ? Don't do that, Lizzie. I won't let ye. You'll never do that for me. I'll chuck meself in the river before I'll let ye do that on my account!'

'Not that, you daft bitch! I'll sing.'

And sing she did. In the middle of Middlesbrough market-place. Stood right in the centre she did, and sang her heart out like a good 'un.

Lizzie made enough money to keep us both over the week-end. Food, enough to put the furniture on the train, and for both our fares back to South Shields. And I've never forgot it.

She was as bold as brass and had a heart as big as a whale.

Well, when I got back, Johnny did like he said and I was put into the Robinsons' lodgin' house in Thrift Street. I was given me own room which I could sleep in if I wanted to, and told to run the whole show. At that time I hadn't the first idea how to manage a lodgin' house.

47

Shortly after that, on Christmas Day, 1909, little Alfie was born. And I had a bad time with him. He was the first baby I'd had in any case, and to make matters worse, the midwife said he was lyin' the wrong way about. The menfolk weren't allowed in at times like that and even if they had been, none of the Robinsons would want anythin' to do with it. The only attention they paid, was when Mr Robinson shouted up the stairs 'Be a brick, Francie, there's a good lass!' and then Johnny shouted after him, 'Aye, that's right, Francie. Be a brick.' Be a brick. . . !

The way I had Alfie was the same as it was to be for each and every one of my bairns. And that was, to work right up to the last minute, till the water broke. Then put a little pile of newspapers in the middle of the room with some clean rags on top and make a little hollow in the middle with me fist. Get somethin' to hold on to—like a heavy chair or a bed-end—and squat down on me heels until it was all over. Afterwards I would just fold over the cloths and paper and that and take it away and burn it. The midwife only came along after it was all over.

None of the Robinsons, even Johnny, seemed at all bothered one way or the other about the new bairn. I suppose the fact that I was on the road with it before I got married, took away anythin' special from it. Mrs Robinson came two days afterwards, and asked is about gettin' it christened. I said I hadn't even thought about it yet. But she insisted that I get it done on the followin' Sunday. So I did, because she said that was the right and proper thing to do when you're a Catholic. Ye had to have it done as quickly as possible, so if it died, it would go to heaven instead of just limbo. The way I had been brought up, was to believe that it didn't look right for a woman to be seen outside of her house too soon after a lyin' in. I wasn't really up to it, because the whole business had taken a lot out of is and I wasn't too steady on me feet. But I went all the same, and with all the standin' around and waitin', I fainted, and the priest had to pour holy water over me to bring is round before he could attend to little Alfie.

The funny thing was, I wasn't christened meself till I was

48

nine or ten years old. We didn't bother too much about that sort of thing in my family. Me mother said she was too ashamed to take us as we had no decent clothes to wear. And she couldn't afford to get me christened because she hadn't a shawl to wrap is in. But when I was older, I saw this poor old lady in raggy clothes gettin' done, and when I told me mother, she took is to the same church and I was done there and then in the clothes I stood up in.

Johnny was now trainin' full time and there was never any more talk about servin' his time, indentures, trades, platin' and rivetin' or anythin' else like that. From now on he was to be a fightin' man and nothin' else. Mr Robinson was to look after his trainin', the meals Johnny was to have, the matchmakin', and all the business arrangements. Deposits, stakes, bettin', the lot.

Even when he was livin' at the lodgin' house with me, Johnny would always go to his father's house for breakfast. Mr Robinson would see to it that Johnny got the proper food and at the proper time. Breakfast was his main meal of the day, but mind ye, like all boxers, he made a feast of it. He'd have bacon, sausages, eggs, tomatoes and onions. And always, most important, the meat to finish up with, on a separate plate. Underdone steak, two inches thick, one day, and leg chops cooked the same way, on the next. 'That's fire in your belly, son. That's where the stamina comes from.' Mr Robinson used to say it had to be bleedin' to do any good. Johnny would have ten minutes rest after his breakfast to let it digest, and then he would be out on the road. He would run for miles. Fast for so far, and then slower. He had to jump as far backwards as he could forwards. His father used to work him hard, as though he was a whippet bein' trained for the track.

After a couple of hours, he would come back to the lodgin' house. He'd have a rub down and a short rest. Then he would be off to Mr Robinson's for sparrin' and skippin' practice. One of the rooms at Mr Robinson's was done out like a proper boxin' trainin' hall, with springs and Indian clubs, punchbags hangin' from the ceilin', and everythin' else what they needed.

49

For a whole month before every fight, Johnny wasn't allowed to see me, let alone share me bed. Usually he was sent to Morpeth to do his trainin' for the fight, to make sure he hadn't anythin' to do with me. Mr Robinson said he couldn't afford to let him get soft. Johnny respected this and I just had to put up with it. However, although his father never knew it, whenever Johnny was trainin' in Shields or close by, he used to creep 'round the back of the lodgin' house last thing of a night-time and tap on the window.

'Are you there, Francie? Are you and the bairn all right? I must be going now. Look after yourself.'

And he was gone.

Every now and then when Johnny was livin' and trainin' at home, Mr Robinson would send round a lump of meat and tell me just how it had to be cooked.

I would do as I had been directed and lay it out for Johnny who would come in, sit down, and wolf it back without even lookin' up.

'Thanks, Francie.'

'Thanks? Thanks! Ye greedy nowt. You've eaten the whole bloody lot, yerself. What about me and the bairn? Are we supposed to sit and starve while you gorge yourself?'

'What do you mean?'

'We've had nowt.'

'Well why didn't you keep your share? How am I to know what you've been eating and what you haven't been eating?'

He would never allow is to see any of his fights, never. Funny, he was never the slightest bit nervous or anythin' about fightin' like ye would have expected. It was just part of the day's work to him. He might just as well have been goin' to the office as to a boxin' match to get his brains bashed out. But I don't think he was really cut out for it. I don't even think he liked it in his heart of hearts. He tried to please his father, but I don't think a man could go that far to please anybody if it wasn't in him already. People used to tell is he wouldn't ever fight in bars. He didn't like brawlin'. He would say, 'There's a proper place for that. If you want to open your mouth, get between the ropes and open it there if you can.' He never mentioned it at home. He was like an ordinary bloke as far as that was concerned.

What a lovely voice he had. In the mornin's before breakfast, I'd be makin' it in the back and I could hear him. He would stand in front of the fireplace combin' his hair. He was daft about his hair. Short at the sides for the boxin' style, but long and dark on top. Lovely it was, and never a single hair had to be out of place.

Anyway, he would sing and sing. In full voice. Loud and sweet. All the lodgers would waken up and listen to him. I was happy then. Fryin' the stuff and mindin' the bairn and just standin' there listenin' to him. He used to sing a thing right through as well. He never started anythin' he didn't finish. I used to think to meself, 'Johnny, you're lovely, and I love ye.' I really, really loved him. I think he knew it as well. I hope he did anyway, because I did. . . .

I once went to see him fight Jerry Delaney. I stood outside and peeped in through a hole. They were goin' at it hammer and tongs and there was blood everywhere. I was shoutin', 'If you mark my man, I'll kill ye when ye come out!'

Course they couldn't hear is in there, there was that much shoutin' and bawlin' goin' on. I was sayin', 'Go on, Johnny, lad! Knock him down! Hit him now! Divvent let him de that to ye! Hit him hard! Now! Now's your chance. Get him! Oh my God. The swine! Me bairn's little bit face! He's all bleedin'. That's it Johnny. Finish him off! Finish him off! Oh That's done it! Oops! What're ye tryin' to do? That's cheatin'! That's right Johnny! Teach him a lesson he'll never forget. Oh I hate this boxin'. . . .'

Mrs Robinson always resented the slight hold I had over her son. Not that she had any cause to worry for Johnny's parents always had their way with him. She would try to make Johnny think I wasn't fit to be his wife or mother to his bairns. She was always supectin' bad things about is and tellin' him. If he listened, he never paid much heed, at least not sufficient to ever say anythin' about it to me. He would just get on with what he was doin' and accept things for what they seemed to him to be.

Late one afternoon, I had took the bairn over to see his grandmother, and Mrs Robinson, in one of her drunken spells, really got stuck into is. She had mislaid a gold sovereign and was bli min' me for havin' pinched it. She was yellin' her head off and tellin' is I was a no good Protestant bastard who was not fit for her son. And much more, besides. Not so much out of fear, but only out of respect for me husband's mother, and knowin' full well that if I were to force the issue Johnny would side with his mother, I quietly went home without sayin' a word. Ye just had to cross her once, and that was it. You were done for.

When Johnny got back to the Robinsons', Geordie had told him what had happened.

'You've got to do something about it, Johnny. It's not fair on Francie. The old woman goes too far. She's always doing it, I can tell you. You don't know the half of it. Francie's a good wife to you, and you should stick up for her.'

And he did stand up for is a little while after when Mrs Robinson started all over again, makin' all kinds of accusements against me, and sayin' I had been sleepin' with the men in the lodgin' house that very day.

'You're a bloody liar, mother. She's been with me nearly all day. We've been out matchin' together. I've listened to you more than enough. Now get out and say no more.'

But she went on shoutin' and ravin' at Johnny. Suddenly he picked her up and threw her on the fire. Luckily for her, it had just been banked up and wasn't bleezin' properly or else she would have gone up in smoke afore she could get her big backside out of the grate. Mind you, it did the trick. She certainly shut up after that.

Johnny said nowt. He just walked away.

But later on when we were in bed that night, Johnny said, 'Don't hate me because of my mother, Francie.' And I said to him that it was all right. I had married him not his mother.

Not long after, little Johnny was born. That was in 1911. And there was no more fuss made over him than there had been over Alfie.

52

6

Lodgin' houses were rough places with tough people in them. Some were ordinary, quite decent and fairly respectable. But nobody went there by choice, only out of necessity. Cheap lodgin's. The only thing they didn't all have to share was the beds they slept in. Still, they were better off in lodgin' houses than they would have been in a workhouse. After all, there was room for a little pride. Here ye paid for all ye got. If ye couldn't pay, ye found yerself in the workhouse. And ye couldn't do just as ye pleased in a lodgin' house. They had strict regulations about how to go on. Every week, somebody in uniform would come round to inspect the premises. Not just an ordinary policeman, but usually a sergeant or somebody pretty high up. They had the power to close a place down if it did not come up to their standards. Many's the time that a little somethin' in the palm has saved somebody bein' put out of business.

The Robinsons' lodgin' houses were much like any others you'd come across. Some were mixed, some were just all men or just all women. I was lucky to be put in charge of a 'Men Only'. Women were always bickerin' and causin' trouble. And ye usually find they are much dirtier in their habits. The state of some of their beds, I wouldn't like to repeat. Little bits of thievin' was always goin' on. They'd be forever pinchin' each other's scraps because they were starvin' hungry. As for the mixed lodgin' houses, well, they were the worst of the lot. Hard to manage for reasons ye can well imagine for yerself. Ye'd always find lodgin' houses in the poor parts of the town. Sometimes a whole street of them, one after the other. Poor people couldn't afford to buy their own houses or even rent rooms. Lodgin' houses had to be. A man only had to be out of work for a few weeks, and that was that. His family would get split up. Him goin' to one lodgin' house, the woman to another, and the kids to the parish. They used to live and hope the bad times

53

would pass and that they could all get together again one day. But as often as not they would all end up in the workhouse.

Dormitories had any number of beds. Twenty in a fair-sized room, ten in a little room, and three or four in a very small one. The rules said that ye could only have as many lodgers as ye had beds, but I would never turn people away on a freezin' cold night with nowhere to go. They could sleep on a mattress if I had one spare, or on the floor with a few blankets. Sometimes they even slept on the kitchen table. I knew if the 'tecs came, me licence would be taken away, but what else could ye do. There was a large dinin'-hall called the eatin'-room, with a kitchen joined on to it. A long, plain, wooden table scrubbed white twice a day with coarse sand, and wooden crackets or benches was all the furniture there was. Pots and pans were provided along with mugs, plates, knives, forks and spoons. I washed them all. A huge fire was always kept bleezin' in the eatin'-room for cookin' and heatin' water. Mostly the wooden floor-boards were bare, but here and there I had little bits of lino to cover the badly worn parts and the stone flags.

At least once a week, on a Friday night, the back yard would be scrubbed, and every day it was swilled down. Off with the shoes and stockin's and out with the pail and long-handled broom. And get on with it.

There was only one door, one way of comin' in and goin' out. And this was kept locked and bolted to stop unwanted people gettin' in, and to make sure that nobody left without payin'.

At first it was fourpence a night but that went down to threepence to keep even with other lodgin' houses that were lowerin' their prices to try and get all the business.

I had me regulars and I encouraged them. They were more reliable and more considerate. Also I didn't have to change their bed linen quite so often. Ye always were supposed to change the bed clothes between lodgers, but if ye saw somebody comin' in who ye weren't too sure about—like if they looked a bit scruffy and a bit drunk, then ye didn't bother too much as long as the bed was straightened up properly.

The canny ones like Johnny Graham and Tommy Fynn

54

would help is with the swillin' and the washin', and keep an eye on me as well. They even helped with makin' the beds and that sort of thing. Me husband Johnny never helped of course. He was too busy with the boxin' and that. He would never interfere if there was trouble either. He would say, 'Get on with it. What would you do if I wasn't here?' Course he was brought up hard that way and knew I'd have to learn to look after meself. He would spar with is some nights when he had time, to toughen is up a bit. I got used to it though and could look after meself pretty well. If they stood up and fit (fought), then I stood up and fit with them. Mind, I was never as good as Mrs Robinson. She could stand up with the biggest and the best of them, man or woman. Fists right up. A big strappin' woman she was and very fierce lookin' when she was roused. Straight down the stairs arse over tip I've seen them goin' down. I would stand me ground unless they were crazy—and some of them were—then, just as they were about to hit is, if I thought they were too strong, I'd run out to fetch the good lodgers if they were in. If they weren't, I'd wait until whoever it was had calmed down, and hoped he would either pay is or just go away. You had to let them see ye weren't afraid of them 'cos you'd get nowhere at all if they thought ye was soft.

I had this old cripple feller who was always wettin' his bed. Sometimes two or three times durin' the day even, though they weren't really supposed to be in their beds before five o'clock. Ye could get into trouble for allowin' it. But when it was cold and ye could see they weren't well, ye couldn't very well go in and tip them out. Anyway, sometimes I was so mad I used to let this feller lie in it all day and try and teach him a lesson. But it was no good. Poor bugger just couldn't help heself, he needed a new washer. He was made that way, I suppose. He used to beg at the door off the lodgers comin' in. Ye weren't allowed to do that either, really. And the other poor souls had nowt of their own. He always used to get somethin' from somewhere or somebody though. I was always findin' these stinkin', sticky coppers in his bed.

Another bloke was supposed to be deaf and dumb, never ever said a word that I can remember from the day he came in.

55

This day however, I heard somebody shoutin' for a pail. I went up, and it was him. He shouldn't have been in the place at all. He must have crept in when I wasn't lookin'. 'Come down here and pay this minute,' I said, 'or ye'll never get out of here alive!' I knew he had money all right. He took off his boot and smashed every single window in the place. All for the sake of threepence. The police heard about it and came for him. I never sent for them. It didn't pay to do that, it got your place a bad name. Poor bugger, they took him outside and bashed him till the blood came out of his ears. I shouted to them, 'Divvent do that to him! Ye'll kill him.' But I suppose they knew what they were doin'. They took him away and locked him up for three months. But he came back as soon as they let him out. We would fall out and fall in again. It was like that.

A rough life, but I liked it. Sometimes at night we'd all get sittin' around the great big fire, lovely and hot. Some of them would sing and talk about all kinds of things. Things that had happened to them and strange things they'd heard about. I liked to listen to them. I only had the bairns and they were very young, and I never saw much of poor Johnny one way or another.

Then there was Foggin. He was dead skinny and lived on 'long pulls'. That was what ye would call a lemonade bottle filled with draught beer. Ye took your empty bottle into the bar and they filled it up from the pump, and ye took it away with ye. There again, ye weren't allowed to drink any liquor on the premises but time and time again I would find him on his bed with the long pulls. I used to shout and bawl at him. 'Foggin, ye great long skinny nowt, I've told ye before. Get out with that or I'll go for ye! Ye'll loss is me licence. He'll say, 'Let's just finish this one, and I'll never have another, ever.' I'd take it off him and pour it out the window, and he'd just sit and watch is, too drunk to do owt. He was strong though, for all he was thin. I've seen him liftin' things very heavy as though they were a bag of feathers. Even if he wasn't drunk he'd just sit there and watch is all the same and beg is not to waste it all. Harmless and hopeless. Many a man would kick you in the belly if ye did that. But Foggin was big, and he was

56

as soft as muck. It would be exactly the same the next night. He just couldn't keep off it. Sometimes I would get so mad, I would knock him about like a football. The other lodgers would stand by and laugh. But he never ill-treated me, I must say that. I put him out several times but he always came back after a couple of months.

Often two men would fight it out and all hell was let loose. Things got knocked over and smashed, stuff spilt all over the floor. It was sometimes better to leave them to get on with it and get it out of their system. But if things were getting too nasty, I used to try and break it up. They once split me head open with a brick. They were sorry afterwards, like. But the damage was done by then.

One time this geet big navvy came in, fleein' around doin' this and doin' t'other. Washin' his shirt and socks, and not payin'. I goes in and says to him, 'You're carryin' on a lot aren't ye? What about weighin' in?'

'I'll weigh in when I think fit.'

'Will ye now? Well you'll not ye know! You'll weigh in now or else you'll get those things up and get out.'

'I can bloody well do that an' all.'

'Well you'd better bloody well do just that.'

I turned round and was just goin' into the kitchen, when he jumped is from behind. He'd took off his great big knobbly belt, clunched it up and was just goin' to smash it over the back of me head when two fellers grabbed his wrist and hoyed him on to the floor. They nearly kicked him to death.

If regulars couldn't pay, well ye let them go for a bit. Sometimes they'd give ye a penny interest or somethin' when they paid ye back, they were so grateful.

I had some funny 'uns in there. There was a lot of quack doctors, 'crocuses' they used to call them, and the things they got up to would turn ye grey overnight. The way they made their medicines. My God . . . most of them wouldn't let ye see how they were doin' it else they would've been locked up. Some of them should have been hanged, let alone locked up. One would mix soap and sulphur up and roll it into little balls in his hand and then wrap them up in silver paper and sell

57

them for rheumatism pills. And their cough candy they used to boil up in pans . . . I never saw them makin' it, they always covered it up. It must have been really bad. Goodness knows how many bairns died eatin' that horrible smelly stuff. Another would buy a pound of foreign beans from the chemist for a shillin'—like little hard pebbles they were—and then sell them as lucky beans or magic beans for one and six each. If they put a thread through to wear round your neck, then it cost ye two bob. Proper bloody frauds they were.

Mind, they never sold the stuff in the lodgin' house. It wasn't allowed and I wouldn't dare let them. Off to the market-place they'd go with their medicines and stuff. They used to mix French chalk from the bike shop with a bit of water and sell it as special toothpaste that would stop your teeth from rottin' and cure mouth sores. There was an Indian dentist that called heself the 'tooth doctor'. He always wore a great big pink carnation. He would say he would pull your teeth out with his finger and thumb. He couldn't even pull his own puddin'. Then they would mix margarine with flour and call them corncakes, 'Only one application, Madame! Only one application necessary!' Aye, only one application and your leg would probably drop off.

They'd shout out for somebody to come up and try their new medicine which would cure anythin'. Epsom salts, vinegar and beetroot juice that was. It certainly looked good in the little bottle with Latin writin' on that nobody could read. I don't know where they copied it off, somethin' they'd seen somewhere that sounded highfalutin'. One of their cronies would come up, doubled up with pain, and screamin' blue murder. He would take one sip of the marvellous medicine and he'd be cured on the spot. It hadn't time to reach his belly before he was completely cured. He would straighten up and wave his arms about laughin' and singin', and run away with the crocus shoutin' after him for his money. All a big show, ye know, but it fooled a lot of people.

Another feller would come up with crutches and throw them away after he'd had a spoonful of somethin' or other. And somebody with his face covered in bandages would tell every-

58

body that he was covered with horrible scabs underneath. Then he would take them off after a drink of the miracle medicine, and his face would be perfect, without a scar. And everybody would gasp out and rush to buy a bottle.

'Will it cure this, doctor? Will it cure that?'

Of course, it would 'cure anythin' from a lisp to an arseful of piles'.

Some of them were good at it though, and had you thinkin'. One bloke used to get a jar of water he'd tinted with some colourin', and he'd get a bit of cord, unravel it, and drop it in. Then he'd go to the market with an old woman and say she had just passed this tapeworm that mornin' after takin' his marvellous purger. Then he would ask them to come up and feel it to see if it was still warm. It would look as though it was movin' and nobody would dare come up and touch it.

Somebody was always runnin' raffles and lotteries that nobody ever won. It was always some lady from Newcastle, or a gentleman from Wallsend who had won last week's prize. When they thought people were cottonin' on to them, they would try somethin' else, or someplace else. They were never stuck for ideas. By, they were fly.

There was one old feller who used to make beautiful flowers out of turnips and carrots, bits of sweet paper and wire. He would cut it all up and dye it, and in a flash he had a lovely bloom that would look a treat in anybody's garden.

One tinker bloke I had, used to go round the scrap-yard for old pans and kettles and do them up. Patch up the holes with chewin' gum and then slap a bit of blackenin' on. He used to rattle like a china shop. He had little tabs inside his coat, and outside, and would tie dozens and dozens of pans on to heself. He was always drunk, and when he came in to go up the stairs he would be for ever fallin' down and bangin' and clangin'. One night I got so sick of him I knocked hell's bells out of him, pans and kettles and all. All his pans were dented and bent, and handles and spouts were lyin' all over the floor. I was sorry for the poor old bugger after I'd done it, but he was a proper bloody nuisance.

We didn't have many coloured fellers in because of the

trouble ye always got, but at one time I had these coal-black darkies for a few days. They seemed quiet and well mannered enough. They had come off a ship and wanted somewhere to stay. Nobody else would take them, so I said I would as long as it was just for a little while. I've never seen anybody so clean. Mind, some say ye can't tell with them. Well, these ones used to have a bath every day and wash their feet at least two or three times. One day I made up me mind to ask them why. They all looked at each other and laughed and the big one says to is in a great big deep voice, 'Well Ma'ma, the reason is 'cos we smell like niggers if we don't.'

They were very hard on ye were the town hall people. Ye had to have your buckets of slops and swill out before nine every mornin', and all your windows open. It wouldn't matter if it was blowin' a howlin' gale and all the windows were frozen up, they still had to be open wide by nine o'clock. All the rooms had to be lime-washed four times a year. That was to keep down the bugs and fleas and that. It was a horrible job. The idea behind it was proper enough but it used to make your hands and arms bright red. And your face, when the stuff splashed on it. Inspectors came and if they saw a matchstick on the floor, they would tell ye to pick it up. Mind, I always kept a very clean lodgin's, everybody said so. But most of the inspectors I had were kind. They wouldn't take any backhanders from me. They would say, 'If you've anythin' for me, Francie, give it to the bairns.'

But one day a new man came. I daresn't offer him his tip in case he had is up for bribery. He looked a queer one, this.

'Scrub this, scrub that! I'm not satisfied with this, I'm not satisfied with that! Do it again, and when you've done it, do it again.'

Every bed-frame had to be scrubbed, be they iron or be they wood. All forty-seven of them. This feller came back day after day. I was really worn out. I said, 'I don't care if ye take the place off is, I cannot keep this up on top of everythin' else. There's no need for it. I'll go somewhere else.' But he had it in for me good and proper. He said even if I got another place he would come and make is do the same. Next time, the chief inspector came, and I told him all about it. 'Find any fault ye can, sir. Go on, have a good look around. I'm at me wits' end.'

'What! This is ridiculous. Don't worry, Francie. I'll see to it this will never happen again.'

He was a real nice man and said he would pull a few strings and get is a smaller place in Holborn. That's the old part of South Shields where the Arabs lived. I said, right. But it cost too much. And later on he told is it was condemned. So it was just as well. All kinds and types of people came into the lodgin' house but they were all the same in this respect, they were down-and-outers every one. Some of them had nobody in the world. Some were separated, widowered, out of work. And some were just rank lazy.

Once this quack doctor came with his son. He was only about fourteen, I think, and small and thin with it. The father sold pills in the market for drink. He used to go away for a while and leave the bairn in the lodgin's. A bonny lad he was. He got on well with my little bairns, and I used to feed him and mother him and look after him when his father was away. I made him feel part of the family. I got him a job as a painter's apprentice and fitted him out with proper apron and boots. But every now and again, his father would take him away, take the clothes off his back, and sell them for his drink. Then he'd send the kid back to me again. Sometimes he wouldn't come home at night for his tea and we would go round all the lodgin' houses and find him as far away as Jarrow or Hebburn or some such place. The other lodgers would help is to find him because they knew I was worried sick about him. I felt responsible for him. He was so little and hadn't much of a life at all. I told the quack I would only give him three more chances. After that they went away and I never saw hide nor hair of them again. So I don't know what happened to the poor bairn.

Old Tommy Fynn was with us a long time. He had been well-to-do once upon a time, but he'd started drinkin' heavy and his family had put him out. I nursed him, and buried him in the end. I did that with four others as well, at different times

61

of course. They weren't allowed to stay in the lodgin' house for more than a day if they were really bad, but I would keep them for more than a week till they got better. Or got worse. Then they would be moved away.

Tommy loved my little Alfie. He used to get him to stay outside his room when he was out, to keep guard, and Alfie would wait there all day full of patience till he came back. It was too much for Alfie, really, because he was very runty. He'd had consumption of the bowels from the day he was born, and his tiny little legs could barely support his bit body, skinny though it was. But I didn't like to hurt Tommy's feelin's because he was so good to the bairn. He would go out in the mornin' with his bundle of rags to sell, and say, 'Now listen here, Alfie, you watch my things and tell me as soon as I come back, if anybody touches anything.' The other lodgers would deliberately take one of Tommy's spuds or a crust of his bread or somethin', to tease him, and Alfie would tell his Uncle Tommy as soon as he came in. In a way, I sometimes felt that truckin' with Tommy Fynn wasn't for the best, but what else could I do? His habit of gettin' Alfie to help fold up the dirty rags he had collected from who knows where, and then share his dinner, used to worry is. He was a good man but he'd let himself go and was not always as clean as he might have been, and the way he prepared his food left a lot to be desired. But I never blamed Tommy and I was grateful for the time he would spend playin' with Alfie where other lodgers would not be bothered with a snotty bairn. And of course his own father was away so much. I never had time to give meself to the bairn as much as I should, even though I wanted to.

It was January, 1913, when Joe was born. His father had been away trainin' and only came back a couple of days before he was born. I was in labour and Johnny brought in a bottle of stout. He says, 'Here, Francie, drink this. It'll do ye good.' I says, 'No, Johnny, ye know I don't drink the stuff.' He took the top off and chucked it all over is. This is what boxin' and trainin' did to him.

As well as sucklin' Joe, I suckled somebody else's bairn as well, 'cos the poor mother had no milk. I did that a few times

62

with different ones. I used to leave off me lodgin' house work and go and feed my bairn and the other woman's at the same time. I would have one at one, and the other at the other.

I was only in bed a couple of days of course for I had little sick Alfie, Joe, and this other bairn to see to. Ye couldn't afford to make a holiday out of it. While I was abed I'd get somebody to fill is a bucket of water and put it on the bed, so's I could wash the nappies.

At that time the rats were very bad. They'd run up and down the curtains and across the bed. I used to pull the sheets over the bairns' faces so the rats couldn't get them while we were all asleep. Ye hear of some horrible things that rats can do to a woman in milk. Every night before she went away, I'd get Mary the servant girl to pass is all the shoes where I could reach them to fling at the rats durin' the night. And when she came back next day, she'd gather them all up again ready for the night-time. Anythin' heavy would do, it didn't have to be only shoes, ye know. She was a good help to me that girl. When I got out me bed, the first thing I did was to get the tongs and poke them down this big hole at the side of the fireplace. Seven, I got out. Seven young 'uns. The big 'uns got away though, they were too sly. I had to nip their bellies in and out with the tongs till they stopped breathin'. They're a lot harder to kill than ye'd think.

Well, after I got up from havin' Joe, little Alfie got so's he couldn't even turn his face round to is, and we had an awful job liftin' him out of his cot so's I could have him on me lap. I says to Mary, 'Mary, if anythin' happened to that poor bairn while I was lyin' here, I think I'd die.'

Just then, the little black crucifix that Alfie had round his neck since the day he was born, jumped off the little silver chain.

'Look Mary, it's come off after all this time. His little cross. You can hardly see our Lord on it anymore. He's all worn away. . . . What a shame. . . . Here, he's lyin' very still, isn't he? There's somethin' the matter with him, isn't there?'

Johnny Graham and Tommy Fynn came in and took the cot away and Tommy was cryin'. 'My little thing's gone. I've nothing to live for now.' From that day forth, Tommy Fynn went down and down. He fretted himself to death, and in less than a year, I had to bury him.

Ten days after baby Joe was born, Alfie was buried in Harton Cemetery. The lodgers clubbed together to buy him a wreath and some of them walked behind in the funeral procession. Johnny did not know what to say, although he tried. Death was one of those things that happened and there was nothin' anybody could do about it.

'Don't upset yourself,' he had said at the graveside, 'there's plenty more bairns to get.'

'You might think so, Johnny. But he's mine. I had him and that's what's upsettin' me. No matter how many ye get, ye always want them all. Every one.'

7

By the summer of 1913, little Johnny was two and a half years old and his father was beginnin' to take an interest in him. We weren't too badly off then. Mr Robinson was lookin' after Johnny's boxin' expenses and a boxer never has to buy his own drink. He just walks into the bar and everybody jumps up. Not that he drank much. I was doin' a bit of bakin' and sellin' it to the lodgers for a few coppers, so I couldn't grumble. On a Sunday mornin' little Johnny and his father would go over to the Robinsons. Big Johnny was proud of his son all dressed up in his purple velvet suit. He looked like little Lord Fauntleroy with his white lace collar pressed down. Spats, white gloves and a little walkin' stick. It was grand to see them struttin' up and down the main street like a couple of peacocks. Big Johnny was very tall and thin and his hand was so high up that little Johnny had to hang on and give a little jump now and again to steady heself. The bairn had to half run to keep up with his father's long quick steps. People would recognise them and go up to them.

'Is this your lad, Johnny? By he's a fine lookin' little feller.'

'Yes, this is my son, my eldest lad. . . . Oh yes, he'll make a good one. I'll see to that. Of course man, I'm making matches for him already. . . . No, nobody famous yet, but one day, you'll see. He'll be Shields' greatest champion.'

One day, a terrible thing happened. Every Friday, I would clean the brasses, and for this purpose, I used to leave the oven door off its hinges to get at the handles. While it was off, I would stack the chopped sticks inside to dry ready for lightin' the fire. This particular Friday, it was rather chilly and so I had changed Johnny into his woollens. Usually he would be in his silk blouse for goin' up to the Robinsons and it was a damn' good job he wasn't this time, or he'd have been burnt to a little cinder.

I had went to the market to get some fish for the dinner, and got on chattin' to the fishwife. One of the lodgers suddenly rushed up to is and said I must come back quickly. I took no notice. They were always fetchin' is because so-and-so had done this, or so-and-so had done that. But he came back again a few minutes later, grabbed me arm and dragged is away from the stall.

'Quick, Francie! It's the bairn! It's little Johnny!'

I dropped me basket on the stall and ran like hell.

Back at the lodgin' house, little Johnny was still smoulderin', wrapped up in a blanket on the floor. All the lodgers were standin' round. Some were pourin' water on him. Some were talkin' to him. Others were lookin' in cupboards for somethin' to put on. What had happened was that when I had gone out, Johnny had started puttin' the sticks in the oven like he had seen me do, and with the oven bein' right next to the bleezin' fire, he had caught alight.

I could smell his burnin' flesh. A lodger called a taxi while I did what I could to make him comfortable. At the infirmary, I insisted on holdin' him meself while they cut away the clothin' and tried to pull out the pieces which had got stuck to the flesh. The trouble was they couldn't make up their minds which was his clothes and which was his own skin. But when he was cleaned up, it didn't look quite so bad. He'd got burns all over

65

his head and body and all his skin was a bright flamin' red. But it was his little right arm that was the worst. This was in a very bad way, and the First Aid people told is it might have to come off.

That night, Big Johnny had come in and asked for some money to go to London for a few days. There was a crowd of them goin' down for the dog races and he needed the fare and money to bet with. I gave it to him gladly and wished him good luck. The lodgers had helped is with little Johnny, because they knew his father would have murdered is if he'd known. We put a clean hankie over the burnt part of his face and then a big scarf right around his head. This was to pretend it was for keepin' the cold out. His long-sleeved nightdress covered the bandages on his body. So it was all hidden for the time bein'.

Johnny was away a week but as soon as he came back, the beans was spilt. Sooner or later he had to know anyway. At first, I thought he was goin' to do is in. But then he saw how upset I was over the whole thing and he just says, 'Well, I know you'll do your best out of a bad job, Francie. I'll say no more about it.' And he didn't either.

I went to the hospital every day, and after a while all the skin dropped off and new white skin grew in its place. But his arm just wouldn't heal up. I brought him home, nursed him meself and took him back for new dressin's every day. For months, day in, day out, I took him, and stood by and listened as he screamed. They were rough and pulled the bandages off with little blobs of flesh stickin' to the lint. They wouldn't allow is into the dressin' room because I always interfered. I was always wantin' to hold him meself, and I didn't know how to hold him properly for the doctor, so they said.

'Don't do that! Be careful with me bairn! Do it the other way! It won't hurt him so much.' I used to start loosenin' the bandages meself before he went in, and they stopped that as well.

'You don't know what you're doing, woman. Leave him to us. We know what's best for him. You're letting the air at it. It's getting more and more infected because of you.' But so

66

tightly was the arm bein' trussed up and tied against his chest, that it became wasted and paralysed. It was less than half as thick as the other one. Big red septic lumps came under both arms.

One day, little Johnny was screamin' and I could hold meself back no longer, so I burst in.

'Gis him here, you bloody butcher! I'm takin' him. I'll look after him meself from now on.'

One nurse had a tight hold on Johnny while the other two pulled is back against the wall and tried to keep is there. The doctor must have heard all the shoutin' and commotion and he came rushin' in. He played war with is, and told is that if I took Johnny away, it would be entirely at me own risk. The hospital wouldn't be responsible in any way and that in all likelihood the arm would have to be cut off and for me to remove him now might kill him.

'He's my bairn and I'm takin' him, mister. You can say what the devil you like, but I'll never bring him back here again, not while there's a breath left in his little body. God gave him that little arm, and I'll see you all in hell, before I'll let you take it away!'

I never went back. I cleaned and dressed the arm meself every mornin' and every night, movin' it up and down from left to right. I would hold out a novelty to make him reach out and then I would pretend I was goin' to take it off him to make him grab it all the tighter. He would try and hide it over his head or behind his back so I couldn't get it. Any spare time I had, I played this game with him even though I knew it was teasin' him.

Once a week, I let me own doctor look at his arm and prescribe some new ointment. Gradually, the skin knitted over the raw flesh which began to get a nice pink tinge to it. His arm filled out and he could move it any way he liked, all by hesel'. A few months later, apart from some awful twisted skin which he always had after that, his arm was pefectly normal.

But even before Johnny's arm got better, he took the measles and they turned into pleurisy and he almost died. I had each and every one of the doctors in, and I was never off their backs.

67

One shillin' and sixpence got two visits and a bottle of medicine and I insisted on me money's worth. I carried him round on a pillow wherever I went, for two weeks. All of a sudden, he was right again. That's the way it is with bairns and their troubles.

I never knew much about the actual boxin'. Only the little Johnny told is when he'd had a few beers and came back in a talkative mood. Or what I picked up from Geordie and Stoker or Charley Whyte, Johnny's trainer.

But by 1913 Johnny was a big name and he was fightin' all over the country—anywhere he could get a good match. He was a very popular man, not only with the boxin' people but with anybody interested in sport. He was a very quiet but friendly man, and never one of those who go round braggin' about havin' done this and havin' done that. He was never afeared of anythin' or anybody and always spoke his mind. To look at him ye wouldn't take him for a boxer. He looked more like an Irish priest.

They used to tell me that to be the best, ye had to be what they call a punisher. Ye had to have a mean streak and never show any mercy in a boxin' ring. Johnny wasn't like that. If he had his man where he wanted him, he couldn't bring heself to finish him off. Everybody liked a knockout, I know that. There was always booin' when somebody won on points. They liked to see a man flat out on his back where he couldn't get up even if he wanted to. Johnny's father used to curse and swear at him when he stood back to let the other feller get up. But although Johnny did nearly everythin' his father told him, that he would not do. Even though it might have meant him goin' on and then losin' the fight.

Mr Robinson would be standin' in his corner shoutin', 'Go on, you stupid bugger. Give it to him now, where it hurts! You've got him! Finish him off!'

They say his movements were beautiful to watch, because he was so quick and so styley. Tradesmen in the market would pawn the shirts off their backs to go and see Johnny fight.

Trainloads of them would travel up to St James Hall at Newcastle when he was on the bill.

There was more fightin' in the lightweight division than in any of the others, so that was the place to make your mark. The limit was nine stones in weight, and Johnny, if left to himself, would have been about eleven or twelve stone. He was always havin' to lose weight. If ye were over the odds at the weigh-in, either ye were disqualified and lost your stake, or ye had to come to some arrangement with the other man's backers. This meant ye got a much smaller share of the takin's. If ye weren't in pink condition, as Johnny called it, ye could get killed in a boxin' ring or have your brains scrambled. Ye not only had to hit the feller, ye had to get out of the way quick before he hit you. In and out, in and out, all the time. Ye had to give the best you'd got. Every time. If ye were fightin' away on foreign ground, ye had to do your best to ignore the other feller's supporters shoutin' and yellin' all the time. Sometimes they had to get the police in if the decision went the wrong way, because the crowd would try to skin ye alive.

On Monday 29 December 1913, Johnny was just twenty-four years old. He had recently beaten Johnny Condon at Newcastle and was out to make a match between the winner of the Delaney-Sterling fight which was to be held that very night. Johnny and his sparrin' partner, Walter Callaghan, were havin' a turkish bath at Northumberland Street baths. Johnny had gone there to take some weight off ready for his fight with Alex Lambert, in January. Walter had told Johnny to come out of the bath in case he sweated off too much—that weakened ye. However, Jerry Delaney was in at the same time and he asked Johnny if he would mind hangin' on till he came out and had his rub-down first, as he was on that night. Johnny said he'd wait on. With the result that he stayed in the steambath too long. I had told him to put his muffler on before he went out that mornin' because it was a cold day. But he wouldn't. By the time he and Walter left the baths, it was snowin' hard. They had called in to the Crown and Sceptre on the way to St James, for a beer and a sandwich. Will Curley,

69

the promoter, who owned the pub, made Johnny put on his fur coat. He told Johnny that he had too much staked on him for the Lambert fight, for him to take any risks. They all went to St James and before the contest, Johnny had jumped into the ring to make his challenge to the winner. That was the way it had to be done. Always before. Never after. When the fight was over, he had a couple of drinks and came home to bed.

The next mornin' Johnny wouldn't get out of bed. Usually when he was trainin', he was up at six o'clock. Otherwise never later than nine.

'C'mon Johnny, get up! It's past your time.'

'I don't feel like it. I'm not gettin' up yet, Francie.'

'C'mon, ye lazy waster. Ye'd better get up. Your Dad'd go mad if he knew you were lyin' there like ye had nothin' better to do.'

'Not yet, Francie.'

'Well I'm goin' over to the lodgin' house to get the men up and chuck out the slops. Them windows have to be open by nine. Be up by the time I get back, and I'll make your breakfast then.'

When I came back Johnny was still in bed.

'What d'ye think you're playin' at? You were drinkin' too much last night, that's what's the matter with you, Johnny Robinson.'

'Would you believe it, Francie, a funny thing happened just before there. I got up when you were at the lodgin' house, to light the fire for you comin' back, and I fell in the fireplace. I felt very queer and sort of weak so I came back to bed.'

'Come on, don't be so bloody bone idle. Get up! Here's your breakfast. Ye'd better get up and get it, I'm not bringin' it to ye in bed. I've got too much to do. It's all right for you just lyin' there without a care in the world.'

Johnny got up and sat at the table but couldn't eat his breakfast.

'Honest, I feel bad, Francie.'

'Don't talk tripe. All the time I've known ye you've never even had a headache let alone owt else.'

But he lay in bed all day and said no more. Next mornin' he

70

still wouldn't get up or eat his breakfast.

'It's a lazy boot you've got, Johnny Robinson. Taken a lazy fit you have. Anybody can see that. Ye'll have to get up to change your underwear.'

'I can't be bothered.'

'Don't be so silly. Howay man, get up!'

He said he still couldn't get up. I didn't know what to make on it so I went off to work and left him. When I came back from the lodgin' house he was delirious, although I didn't realise it for the life of me.

Before leavin' that mornin', I had told him that he had better not fall asleep. His gold watch was in the pocket of his jacket which was hangin' on the back of the bed, and the lodgin' house was just across the road. Ye had to be very careful.

When I came back at half past three, I saw his watch was missin' from his jacket. I looked all over for it but couldn't find it. I shook him.

'Where's your watch? It's all we've got that's worth anythin'. Has anybody been in?'

Johnny stared at is and he had a crazy look in his eyes that I've never seen before.

'It's all right, Francie. Come here, little Francie, it's all right. Quick, give me your hand! Put your head in here and feel this funny noise. Look in here!'

With that, he reached out and grabbed is by the neck and stuck me head under the bedclothes and rammed me face into the mattress.

'Don't be so silly, Johnny, you're hurtin' is. Where's that bloody watch?'

I found it tucked away beneath the mattress. It was still tickin'.

By teatime he was pullin' the frills off the quilt and tearin' the feathers out of the pillow and scatterin' them all over the room. After a while he seemed to quieten down so I went out to borrow some wine glasses. It was New Year's Eve and people would soon be comin' in for their drink. Many friends would be callin' to wish Johnny all the best for 1914. Soon a

71

gang of his pals and relatives had gathered and their drinks were poured out for them.

All of a sudden, Johnny stood up and shouted.

'All you fellers'll have to go. Now!'

Johnny ordered everybody out except his father. It was not even midnight and they hadn't even finished their drinks. By midnight, Johnny had gone mad. Mr Robinson sat on a wooden chair by the side of the bed. He was very still and said nothin' as Johnny raved and sang. Johnny's voice was always so sweet and soft, but now it had taken on such a wild note that as I hurried through the dark wet streets to fetch the doctor, I could hear it as clearly as if I had been in the room with him.

As more and more of his friends called, Johnny would stop singin' and ask them, 'Have you got a tanner? I'm saving up to marry our Francie. I'm getting married, you know. Oh yes, we've decided. Howay, give me a tanner for my wedding!'

Dr Dalziel came and told me that Johnny was only sufferin' from a heavy cold, and that I had to keep him in bed and put hot poultices on his chest. More people kept callin' all the time, and as fast as I was showin' them out, others would be pushin' their way in to see Johnny. All night long this went on. In the mornin', Johnny was quiet, and sleepin'. And soakin' with sweat. He seemed a bit better, and Mr Robinson went home after promisin' is that he would be back soon. And he was. Right through Johnny's sickness, except for a few trips home to check on his own lodgin' house, Mr Robinson sat in the corner of the room where his son lay. All Thursday I was keep puttin' hot flannel poultices on Johnny and rubbin' him with olive oil. The kettle was kept on the boil all day. At one time Johnny leaped up and said, 'If you put another one on me as hot as the last one, I'll clap it on your face!'

I just laughed at him. He must be gettin' better at last. But by the Friday, he was worse than ever. One minute he was quietly sleepin'. The next he was out of his mind. I had all three of the doctors in in turn, but they all said the same thing and prescribed the same treatment—poultices, poultices, poultices.

72

Me and Charley Whyte nursed Johnny as best we could with Mr Robinson lookin' on, doin' nothin' and sayin' nothin'.

Durin' the Friday night, there was a tremendous bangin' on the door which went on for several minutes. Charley Whyte opened the door and looked outside but there was nobody there. He had just sat down when there was a sound of shatterin' glass. Just like the sound glass makes when it's smashed hard against a stone. The globe of the gasmantle which was still alight and all together, had millions of tiny cracks in it. But not one single splinter fell either then, or afterwards.

On the Saturday, Johnny was just the same. By night-time I was exhausted. Mr Robinson spoke. 'Go next door and rest your eyes, Francie. I'll watch him.'

So I went into Lily and Stoker's. Lily was Johnny's sister.

I couldn't sleep there, I just sat at the table with me head in me hands, and started to cry. Somethin' was wrong. Somethin' was seriously the matter with Johnny. I knew that now. Suddenly I heard somebody shoutin' 'Quick, get the doctor, somebody.'

I rushed back. Mr Robinson looked as though he'd been in a scrap, and looked badly shaken up. Johnny's friends had been callin' all the time and six of them had only just managed to stop Johnny from stranglin' his father. They had sent for a strait-jacket but Mr Robinson wouldn't allow them to strap Johnny in it. Even though they insisted it was for his own good.

I raced back to the doctor's house. I grabbed the speaker outside the front door and shouted up.

'Doctor, can you come to Mill Street straight away. Me husband is very poorly! It's serious this time!'

'Mill Street? It's no good me coming down. I can't do anything for him.'

'What d'ye mean? Please come, doctor.'

There was no answer.

A young feller was standin' by, waitin' to call on the doctor's.

'Please, mister, I'm in such a state I don't know what he just said. Will you ask for is? Quick! Please be quick. It's me man, Johnny Robinson. He's very poorly, mister.'

73

He got told the very same thing.

I ran all the way back home.

When I got there, there was nobody there except Mr Robinson. He was still sittin' by the bed, very quiet. Feathers and bed linen were torn to shreds and scattered all over the room. The brass bedstead was twisted up. Spars had been snapped, the knobs pulled off and flung away. Johnny was hangin' over the bed. Only his legs were still covered.

I heaved and dragged him back into bed. Mr Robinson seemed to be watchin' is.

While I was out at the doctor's Johnny had apparently got up and stood in front of the mirror and very carefully combed his hair. Then he had asked for a glass of water, drank it, bit a lump out of the glass, spat it out, got back into bed. And died. It turned out that he had had double pneumonia.

And all that time his mother didn't even call once. She was on one of her Rantans. That was when she used to go nobody knows where, and drink gin for days on end.

8

Well, I began to tidy up. I rolled up me sleeves and swept and cleaned. All night I swept and swept, cleaned and cleaned, shiftin' things round, puttin' them back and shiftin' them again. As soon as it was daylight there was a knock on the door and in came the handywoman.

'What do you want?' I says.

The handywoman walked to the bed and pulled away the pillow from under Johnny's head, and straightened him out.

I saw what she was doin' and rushed to the bed and felt Johnny's face.

'Oh, Johnny, Johnny, Johnny! Me Johnny! Oh me Johnny! It's true. . . . It's really true! You've gone, Johnny, haven't ye? Oh . . . Johnny.'

Mr Robinson just sat very still in the corner lookin' on all this time.

74

'What'll I do, Dad? What ever am I goin' to do now?'

'Francie, I've got three daughters. One is good, one I won't mention and one is special. And the special one is you.'

'Don't say them things, Dad. They're all your bairns. They're all your flesh and blood just the same.'

'Yes, I know, Francie. But take my word for it, you'll be better off as a widow than as a wife. And I'm not saying that because I don't love my son, you know that. You look after the business the way you are now, and as for the two bairns, they can come to the Model Lodging House and help me with the books when they get on a bit, and I'll see them all right.'

It was Sunday mornin' and by now Charley Whyte came in with the priest who was very upset and kept apologisin' over and over again. Then I realised that he mustn't have given Johnny his Last Rites. The day before somebody had fetched him but he hadn't thought Johnny was poorly enough to give them to him then, and now he was sorry. But it was too late for anythin' like that now.

'Well, it doesn't matter now, Father. Anyway I don't think he was such a bad man that he'll be put in hell.'

Mr Robinson said he was goin' next door for a lie down in Stoker and Lily's for a little while.

'Now you've no need to worry about a thing, Francie. I'll pay for everything. Just get whatever you want for the funeral, and I'll see to it.'

Just then, Mrs Robinson came in with Mary Ellen and Mr Robinson turned on her.

'You're no mother at all. You've been so bloody drunk for so long that you didn't even know the lad's been bad, never mind dead and gone. I'm taking my name off the door. I'm not having it up beside yours any more.'

When they had all gone, nobody else came.

That was the finish now. Exceptin' old Mrs Hancock from the market. She brought me a sandwich and a pot of tea up. The only thing to heat with in the room was the fire, so I couldn't even boil a kettle. I daresn't light it in case it would turn poor Johnny. I had already poured two bottles of whiskey down his throat, but he was still turnin'. Later on Geordie came to see his brother, but he only stayed a little while. The Robinsons seemed as if they couldn't cope with the situation. They didn't seem to know about sickness or bother much about death.

Durin' the days Johnny lay in that room waitin' to be buried, hardly a soul came near the place. He was dead, and everybody had to deal with it in their own way. I hardly knew what I was doin' or what day it was as I waited with him for the hours to tick away. I just slept in a chair because the bed had been taken down to make room for the flowers and wreaths which arrived by the score.

Some people must have thought we had plenty of money because Johnny was a prize-fighter. Eighteen pounds was all we had saved from our share of the takin's. The promoters and backers were the ones who made the big money. Johnny certainly never got what was shown on the bills. The night after Johnny died, a man kept bangin' on the windows and doors sayin', 'Open that door, open the door. I've got something to tell you.'

It was a strange voice to my ears, and I kept shoutin', 'Go away, go away. Leave me alone, will ye.'

For an hour or more he knocked and banged louder and louder until at last, big Ginger Porter, the policeman, heard him and grabbed him by the neck, took him to the top of Thornton Stairs. Turned him upside down, shook him until all the money fell out of his pocket, and then kicked him all the way down again.

'Open up, Francie. It's all right, pet. It's only me, Ginger, the constable. Get the bairns to pick up the coins in the morning. Keep them. They're yours.'

The next night somebody else came doin' the same thing. I knocked through the fireplace to waken Stoker who came rushin' out, but whoever it was had gone off into the dark. The third night and the same thing happened again. It was gettin' on me nerves by now, so I thought, 'I'll have them, or they'll have me. I'll tackle ye on me own this time, ye swine!'

So sayin', I rushed out into the pitch black with the poker. I struggled with him and hit him, and as he came into the doorway, his face was familiar. I dropped the poker and clawed at his face with both hands and me hands became all sticky. He chucked is down and ran away.

'Where have I seen that face before? Where have I seen it. . . ? Johnny! That's it! I've seen him hangin' round Johnny with the boxin' crowd.'

Next day I found out where he lived and went to his house. His wife answered the door.

'Is your husband in. . . ? Well get him!',

'What for?'

'Get him! I'll sharp tell ye what for all right. Go on, I want to see his ugly face.'

When he came he said, 'I'm sorry Francie. I didn't realise it was you. . . . I thought it was somebody else. . . . I thought. . . . I'd had a few beers and I. . . . I must've got lost. . . . Honestly I. . . .'

'See the sod's face, missus? Him! He tried to get me last night, he did. The bloody swine!'

'I've told you, Francie. I made a big mistake.'

'You made a bloody, very big mistake, mister. And if you ever make a one like that again at my door, I swear it'll be the last mistake you ever make!'

The funeral procession left from my house at two o'clock on Wednesday 7 January 1914, and passed through the main streets of South Shields. They were lined with people, ordinary people who had admired Johnny Robinson as a boxer, and loved him as a man. It was the biggest funeral Shields had seen for a very long time. All of the boxin' and sportin' public were there. Landaus pulled by black horses took my Johnny to the cemetery at Harton. The reception was at the Robinsons' house and me and the bairns were supposed to stay there for the followin' week until I had pulled meself together and could get things sorted out.

Mrs Robinson said the best thing would be for me to put the bairns, Johnny and Joe, in her hands and that she and their grandfather would bring them up while I was workin'.

'No thank you, Mrs Robinson. They're my bairns and Johnny's bairns, and I'll bring them up in my own way.'

That night I was sittin' in the kitchen sucklin' Joe.

'Geordie, ask your mother for a pot of cold tea when she's finished, will ye? What with all that's happened this week, I'm not makin' sufficient milk for this bairn.'

Geordie did as I bid him, but Mrs Robinson was still mad about me turnin' down her offer to look after the children.

'Ahht! Give the bitch a jug of piss, it'll do her just as much good!'

I packed me things and went back to me own home with the bairns, that very night.

Five days later Mr Robinson was dead. The Big Man's heart had broken at last.

By the time he had got back from Johnny's funeral, he was ill. Ye could see it in his face. The next day he'd took to his bed. First thing in the mornin' after openin' the lodgin' house windows and emptyin' the night's slops, I would go over to see him. And then again when I had finished me work. I would rub his chest with mustard ointment. And wipe his face and hands with a damp cloth. Then I'd give him a drink of hot milk. This day, I says to him, 'I'll have to go out to buy a black hat or I'll never be able to show meself now that I'm a widow. I'll have to get one out of respect for Johnny.'

'Where are you going to?' he says.

'Just to Mordains in Frederick Street. I'll not be long.'

'Then turn me over before you go, so that I'm facing Johnny. I feel nearer to him on the other side.'

He was very hard to shift, him bein' twenty stone or more. But I climbed on the bed and moved him sufficient so he was content.

'Right, I'll have to go now Dad, or they'll be closed.'

'Well, you'd better give me a kiss before you go, because I won't be here when you get back.'

'Now don't talk like that, Dad. You're only sayin' that. You'll pull through sharp enough.'

By the time I got back, he'd gone. Pneumonia. Again.

With him gone, I was really out on me own. He had been a hard, big, good man. And I had loved and respected him. Now for it. I was sent Johnny's funeral bill on Mrs Robinson's say-so and told to pay it by meself.

A few days after, on a bitterly cold day, I visited Johnny's grave for the first time, with a few flowers in me hand. I had both me two bairns with is. Both of them under three years. Me eyes lit up when I saw the beautiful headstone that had been put up to Johnny and I came round to the front to read it.

JOHN
dearly beloved son of
Henry and Sarah Robinson
Who died Jan. 4th 1914
Aged 24 years

Me eyes filled with bitter tears as I read the words over and over again. Nearby, a man was standin'.

'I know what you're thinkin', missus. I'll help you put one up yourself. You don't know me, but I knew Johnny very well. I made a lot of money out of backing him.'

I thanked the man for his offer, said 'No thanks', and never saw him again.

With Johnny gone, Charley Whyte, his old trainer, had become a proper nuisance. He thought the sun shone out of Johnny Robinson, and would do any mortal thing for him. He had been a humpyback from birth, but funnily enough he loved sports. Particularly boxin'. So when he got in with Johnny, he was over the moon. Even though he was made like he was, Mr Robinson said he was a damned good trainer. He always kept himself very fit although he couldn't do any fightin' of course. He knew all there was to know about boxin'. All the famous men, past and present. All the ins and outs of the game. He liked the matchmakin' and all the talkin' that went on as well as the big fight itself. He wouldn't allow Johnny to let up for a single minute. They say he was a marvel at puttin' bones and joints right. And he was a natural massager. It was funny to see him followin' Johnny about. Always hangin' round 'im he was. But what really counted with me was the way he looked after Johnny when he was dyin'. Charley

79

waited on him hand and foot. I know that he loved him.

Afterwards, I bought Charley a suit for the funeral as he had nowt decent to wear. It was only a second-hand one, for about twelve bob. And I gave him money for drink even though I could ill afford it. It was the only thing that seemed to help. He would be about forty when Johnny died and Johnny and me were all he had in the world. However, after Johnny died, Charley felt he had the right to move in where Johnny left off. In every way. When I realised what he was up to, I had to put him out of the lodgin' house altogether.

A bit later, when I had me little shop, I would be servin' me customers when Charley would walk straight in and demand his order there and then without waitin' his turn. And if I didn't give it to him right away, he would stamp out of the shop. Later on, I would parcel up what he had wanted, and take it up to him. But he wouldn't take it then and would clash it down and go off in a huff. Then he started followin' is whenever I went out, and asked questions if ever he saw is talkin' to any man. It got so that he was gettin' on me nerves. I was very grateful to him for what he'd done for Johnny. But that was all. I had been tryin' to make a go of the little shop at the time, lookin' after the lodgin' house and me own bairns. And he was just too much on top of all that. He got more and more jealous, and I got more and more fed up with him. But a few weeks after I'd put him out, he lost his senses. I brought him back to nurse him. For five days I kept him. But in the end I couldn't cope no more and I had to have him taken away to the madhouse. Soon after that he died and they sent for me to bury him. I was the nearest thing to a relative that he had.

In just over a year, I lost me son, me man, and me father. I know Mr Robinson wasn't me real father but he was more of a one to me than me own had ever been. First little Alfie, then Johnny, and now Mr Robinson. Things had been hard enough before, but at least Johnny had brought some money in. He would never interfere in any trouble at the lodgin' house, but knowin' that he was never very far away had made me feel safe. It was because everybody knew I was married to Johnny Robinson that stopped them from tryin' to do things that they

80

might of thought about doin'. After all I was a young woman, alone amongst all those men. And men are men, no matter what their callin'. I knew I could expect nowt from Mrs Robinson. And I couldn't turn to me own family. They were worse off than me.

The rooms me and the bairns lived in were owned by the Robinsons. So were the lodgin' houses that I looked after. They charged me sixteen shillin's a week rent but from the two furnished rooms I let out, I got eight shillin's each. So that paid for the rent. There were forty-seven beds in the Thrift Street Lodgin' House, and they all cost threepence a night. If a lodger paid a full week in advance, he got one free night, bringin' his rent down to one and six for the week. Out of this, I had to find all the lodgin' house expenses: a hundredweight of cinders every day of the year, firewood, cookin' things, cutlery, crockery, cleanin' stuff, beddin', and laundry. Out of what was left, me and the bairns lived.

Things were very tight then, and as I walked the cobbled streets to the lodgin' house every day, I felt as though the very stones under me feet were turnin' against is. I was lonely with only the bairns for company. It was very cold, it was dark, and it was always rainin'. The days seemed without end. And so did the nights. But as I walked, as I scrubbed, I thought and I planned. Not for the future, that would have to take care of itself in due course, but for the present. How to feed and clothe the bairns and bring them up decent. I had no time for talkin' or playin' with them much though I'd like to. Or for takin' them to the park or anythin' like that. The most important thing was just to keep them alive. Nobody was goin' to take my bairns away. Not over my dead body. I'd just have to hope that when they grew up, they'd understand why they didn't get all the things they'd wanted. I would bring them up to be honest and decent and hope that God would take care of the other things.

After Johnny died I wrote to wor Nellie to tell her. She had emigrated to Canada in 1911. She had joined Sep who'd gone out two years before, before Johnny and me were married. It

81

F

seems Sep had a very good job out there and that they were both doin' very well. For the past five years, Nellie had been sendin' postal orders to wor JaneAnne to help to keep me father. He was still livin' with JaneAnne and Jim Kilcaldy. Nellie also sent me the odd postal order from time to time, although I never asked for it. I always used to write and tell her that I was doin' fine. I knew she worried about me with bein' the youngest. When she got me letter she straightaway wrote back tellin' is to come to Canada. She made it sound like heaven on earth. She says I wasn't to do anythin' but wait till she had made all the necessary arrangements. These things take a long time, but she would do it. And pay me fare out there and everythin'. And I just had to rest easy and leave everythin' up to her. It seemed like a good chance to make a fresh start in life. And so I said yes, I would come.

In the meantime I heard that me sister Lizzie was goin' from bad to worse. In and out of the workhouse she was goin'. So I made up me mind to find out where she was livin' and then go and see her. I found her in Middlesbrough and she seemed to be goin' crackers. She had taken up with this feller who didn't do much work. Somethin' to do with the Church but I don't rightly know what. They had too many bairns. And some of them scattered all over. Some looked after by one and some by t'other. What a mess she was in. Mind I'll say this much, she might have been filthy and she might have been bad, but she was one of the hardest workers I've ever come across. Always man's work she did. Fetchin' and carryin' at the docks or at the brickyards. She was a brickie's labourer there for a long time. And that's hard work for a woman.

Anyway, I managed to get her on her own, and I says, 'Are you married to this feller, Lizzie?'

She says, 'Yes.'

I says, 'Where then? Where were ye married?'

She says, 'That's my business.'

I says, 'Look, Lizzie. That's your business all right, but surely to God you're not livin' in sin again? If he's a widower like ye say he is, why can't ye get married?'

I could see I was wastin' me time and that I could get no

more out of her. So I said I'd take Maggie, her eldest daughter, who was twelve. I'd feed her and I'd clothe her and she could look after my bairns while I was workin'. I could do extra work over and above the lodgin' house if she'd mind Joe and Johnny. That way we'd all benefit by it. She agreed. So I brought Maggie back to Shields with is.

For a while now, I had been gettin' in the odd stone of flour and makin' little buns which, added to a teaspoonful of tea and milk—just enough to make a pot of tea—I sold for a penny, to the lodgers. More often than not they couldn't afford to buy a full packet of tea or a bottle of milk, or the ingredients to cook with. But they could scrape up a copper or two to buy my little all-in-for-a-penny packets. These went down very well, so I started gettin' off-cuts of beef and other cheap but tasty food scraps from the market, makin' bowls of good thick soup, and sellin' it by the basin. Soon, people from outside the lodgin' house heard about me cheap but good food, and they began to come with their pennies and their basins. This little sideline was doin' really well and so I began makin' what ye called 'threeha'penny starvers' and other such things that looked nice and tasted good. The 'starvers' were dry oven-bottom bread sandwiches with a slice of cornbeef. And they were more popular than anythin'.

After a few months of this, things were beginnin' to pick up, when this feller Lizzie was livin' with, turned up at the lodgin' house. He was askin' for money to buy the bairn (he meant for an abortion). I asked him if it was wor Lizzie, and he said, 'No it's one of mine.' I told him to go to one of his own relations. Then he said it was wor Lizzie. I picked up a kettle that was boilin' on the fire and I rushed up to him with it and said that if he didn't get out and come back no more, I'd pour the scaldin' water all over him. He went away. But shortly after, Lizzie came back askin' is for money and threatenin' to take Maggie away. In the finish I let her go with the bairn and the few clothes that I'd bought. And with the few shillin's I'd put aside in a money-box for Maggie. I never gave her no pocket money, but I had been strivin' to save somethin' for her for when she'd need it. Lizzie took the lot and I never saw her again for a long long time after that.

Shortly after, war broke out and that drowned me hopes of goin' to Canada. Nellie wrote to say that although she had done everythin' she said she would, it was too dangerous to get on a boat then. Anyway the Navy was takin' over all the shippin' so I probably couldn't have gone even if I'd wanted to.

There was an old cobbler's shop joined on to the lodgin' house. I thought to meself, 'If only I could get that shop, I could do me own bakin' and sell it in the window. And as well as that, I'd be able to buy bags of flour, tea and sugar, and a few other basic groceries which could be split up into small lots and sold in little bags that ye couldn't buy anywhere else.' Most shops wouldn't be bothered with sellin' by the teaspoonful. Or bother with anybody only wantin' a couple of slices of bread. But I certainly would. An old lady called Mrs Prince had a busy little general dealer's shop just across the road and she rented the old cobbler's shop as a store. I think she must have known what was on me mind, because one day when we were chattin' on, she said, 'The little cobbler's shop would be just right for you, Francie. I'm an old woman and can't be bothered much longer. I've got a good business going for me across the road and don't really need the cobbler's shop as well. There are lots of odds and ends that would be just the job for you to start off with. There's scales, bins, plenty shelves and a few sacks of potatoes. Lentils, flour. You could take it all to give you a good start. I won't be needing it.'

'What about yerself, Mrs Prince? Won't it spoil you if I start opposite? That won't be fair to you.'

'Look, hinny, you need the money, I know that. I've got enough to get me by. Anyway, I'm not doing the sort of stuff you're going in for. We won't clash, don't you worry, pet. Being so close to the docks and with all these pubs around, there's more than plenty for both of us.'

'Eeh, thank you very much, Mrs Prince. How much will you be wantin' for it? For everythin' in the shop, I mean?'

'Let's see. . . . Eight pounds. . . . Is that all right for you?'

84

'That's fine. I'll away for the money and come straight back. I'll ask Mrs Robinson to lend is it. After all, it's for the good of her own grandbairns.'

But Mrs Robinson refused to lend is the money and asked where on earth did I think she could lay her hands on a sum like that, in ready cash.

'I can really make a go of it, Mrs Robinson, I know I can. If ye can only lend is it, I'll pay it all back as soon as I'm able. You'll see, as sure as God's me judge, I will.'

She wouldn't be budged though, and so I went back to tell Mrs Prince that I had decided not to take the shop after all.

'Why, what's the matter, Francie? Only this morning you said there was nothing in the world you wanted more than that little shop.'

'I know, Mrs Prince, but I've thought it over and changed me mind since then.'

'Oh come on now. I know you're not being perfectly honest with me, are you? It's too much for you. That's it, isn't it? I can tell. Look, Francie, do you really want it? Say yes, or no. Now I want the truth, do you hear?'

'Oh, Mrs Prince, I would love to have it if only I could get the money for it.'

'You can have it then. If you like you can pay me so much a week, or nothing at all. It doesn't make any difference to me, dear. I don't really need the money.'

So I gratefully took the shop and in next to no time it was thrivin' well. Not a goldmine, but somethin' worth workin' at.

After I had finished me duties in the lodgin' house, I would go into the shop takin' with me the buns which had been bakin' while I had been doin' the chores. Then I would make up the small allocations from the bulk stocks in little paper cones, ready for me customers. Gradually I increased me stocks in larger amounts to get me discount. And I was soon able to sell larger bags of this and that to those people who didn't have to live quite so much from hand to mouth.

Business was good. The Robinsons even shopped there. But they ran up so much credit that I had to call a halt, and they

85

did not take too kindly to that.

By the beginnin' of 1915, the war was well under way and they were callin' people up all over the place. Geordie Robinson and Stoker Allan were sent abroad. And them that weren't had to work in factories makin' guns and bombs or somethin' like that to help we win the war. 'Course, there were always some who found excuses not to go and do their stint. And those were the ones who did themselves good. They must have been pretty thick-skinned though because people round-abouts used to hate them. If their menfolk were away gettin' killed, they didn't see why other people's shouldn't be doin' the same. The women used to get themselves really worked up. They would call them cowards and yeller-bellies to their faces. The conchies used to get sent the white feather to show them up. My man was dead, and me bairns were too young, so I was lucky I suppose.

I remember the night a big crowd smashed up Siebers' pork sausage shop in the market. They were Germans, and though they were canny people, they got it in the neck. They were yellin' and shoutin' and screamin' and I felt sure somebody'd get killed that night. I don't know what happened to the rest of the family, but Mrs Sieber got away and came knockin' on my door. I wished to God she hadn't because I didn't know what they'd do to me if they found her at my place. I wanted nothin' to do with it. I didn't think it was right to go for the Seibers and take it out on them. But I was English and I didn't like the Germans either. They were our enemies after all. Any-way, I let her in and she stayed the night. By next mornin' the gangs had gone and so she went away to some relatives some-where. And I never saw her again.

9

On 21 July 1915, Johnny's sister, Mary Ellen Robinson, was married to Walter Callaghan, Johnny's old sparrin' partner. As always, the reception was at the Robinsons'. Mrs Robinson had made a big splash of the weddin', and there were hundreds of people there. Most of them boxers by the look of them. This suited Mrs Robinson right down to the ground. Her youngest daughter was marryin' a boxer, and a Catholic. She couldn't have prayed for anythin' more than that.

The Callaghans of Jarrow were well known as fighters. Walter had fought Jimmy Wilde, the Champion, at Newcastle the year before. His brother Tommy was an all-rounder. Boxer, runner, footballer, cricketer and wrestler. They used to call him the Iron Man of Jarrow, but his fightin' name was Stoker Callaghan, and only his friends called him Tommy. Their eldest brother went by the name of Jack O'Callaghan. When the father, old Tom O'Callaghan, had come to Jarrow, he and his wife, Jane, who was a schoolmistress, decided to drop the 'O' from their name. There was a lot of ill-feelin' towards the Irish, and he thought his bairns would stand a better chance in life if people thought they were English. Well, all of them kept to it except Jack. When he grew up, he put the 'O' back in his name and wore it ever since. He said, 'If I'm born O'Callaghan, then O'Callaghan it shall be. It's a good enough name for me.'

Mrs Callaghan was a real live-wire. Always talkin' and busyin' about. But Mr Callaghan was the quietest man I ever met. In fact I can't ever remember hearin' him speak at all. Whenever ye came into the room, where he was, he would get up and walk out. He wasn't rude or anythin'. Just very shy I suppose. Always his head was burrowed in the Bible.

At the weddin' party they kept pushin' Jack O'Callaghan at me, and me at him. Mrs Robinson was the main one. She kept sayin', 'Go on, Francie. Go over and talk to Jack O'Callaghan. He's a nice feller. Just suit you, he would. Make a good Catholic father for the bairns.'

'I didn't come here seekin' a husband, Mrs Robinson. I came for the weddin'.'

'Well then, don't be so daft. This might be the makings of your own. Go on, get after him.'

This was the first time I'd ever clapped eyes on Jack O'Callaghan. He had a mass of curly hair and was quite good-lookin'. And he seemed a canny enough feller. Nicely spoken and polite. But he was no Johnny Robinson. And nobody could fill Johnny's place as far as I was concerned.

Though I say it meself, I wasn't bad to look at. At twenty-six, I was in me prime. I was big, and I had plenty of colour. I had lovely long brown hair and I don't think I'd have wanted for attention if I'd wished it. The trouble was, people thought I had a lot more money than I really had, just because of the shop. After all, it was only very small and didn't do much more than pay its way. Some folks seem to think if ye don't go round pleadin' hard up all the time, ye must be well off. It wasn't that way with me. It was just that I wasn't given to goin' round moanin' all over the place.

A few days after the weddin', Jack O'Callaghan called at me little shop in Thrift Street. He said he'd come to buy a packet of Woodbines and asked to see the bairns. Every few days he would come with a packet of sweets for them, or a little toy. Then he began to call every day. Never to see me, so he said, only the bairns. He would take them on his back and crawl around the floor, play games with them and chase them around the yard. Sit them on his knee and tell them stories. They loved it. I could see that they needed a father to take an interest in them. Someone who could guard them and look after them. I knew inside that Jack just wasn't my type, but I had to admit to meself he was good for the kids. Sometimes I would think of the value of havin' a man always about the house. And what would become of the kids if anythin' happened to me? Times were hard and people were rough. I had known meself what it was to grow up without a proper father. Two workin' would double the incomin's, and double the money that could be spent on food and homely comforts. It would double the boys' chances of livin' long enough to be men who could be proud and stand on their own two feet. And not owe nobody nowt.

A woman on her own with kids, was no better than a loose woman in many people's eyes. A man on his own was on his own because he had left a bad match, a no good, idle woman. Or a slut. Who was to know that he was married and separated

88

anyhow? But not so with a woman. And who was to know if she had ever even been married at all?

In no time at all Jack O'Callaghan was stayin' to all hours and I had a lot of work to get on with. I'd be tired, I'd be busy, and in any case I've never had no time for idle chatter.

'Haven't you got a home to go to, Jack O'Callaghan? Instead of stayin' here to all hours of the night?'

'I only came to see if the bairns were all right.'

'I know that, Jack, and I appreciate it. But they've been in bed long since, and it's high time you were goin'. I've got some sewin' to do and lots of little bits of things that I can't get on with when you're sittin' there.'

'I love you, Francie, I want to marry you, woman. That's why I'm here now. I've been waiting for a chance to talk to you by yourself.'

'Now if that's the way ye feel, Jack O'Callaghan, you'd better go. And ye needn't come back neither. I certainly don't love you and I never could. I hardly even like ye. I think far too much of the husband I lost to think about anybody else. So don't keep follerin' me round for the love you think I can give ye.'

'If only you'd marry me, Francie, love would come. I know. It would grow. You'd see I'd look after the kids. Anybody can see they need a father.'

'You're not their father, Jack O'Callaghan, and ye never will be. They're my Johnny's bairns.'

'Yes, but I could try and take his place. They need somebody to protect them when you're at the lodging house. Somebody to protect them at night. And you, what about yourself? It's very dark at nights and this is a rough area. You don't know who's hanging about. All those foreign seamen coming out of the pubs and them black niggers coming out of doorways when you least expect it. I've got a good job at the munitions factory and am getting a pretty good wage. All that would be for you and the kids. What with the war and all that, times are going to get harder and harder. All the papers say that. And if anything happened to you, what would become of the bairns? Mrs Robinson would take them. You know that full well. She wouldn't let them go to the Charity. And she can be pretty tough as you well know, Francie. A grand old woman, maybe. But not soft on them like you or I would be. What about it, Francie? Just give me the chance to prove it to you and you'll see that all I've been telling you is the gospel truth. All I'm asking is that you'll think it over. All right? Now that's not much to ask is it? So I'll not ask for an answer now. Do you think that you will though, Francie?'

'No!'

Well, he pestered and pestered so much, along with all the rest of me relatives, that I wondered if I was right in keep sayin' no. And then it happened that if he missed comin' for a day or so the bairns were askin' for him. So in the end, for their sakes, I said yes.

On 9 February 1916, Jack O'Callaghan and me were made man and wife. I was lookin' after the Thrift Street Lodgin' House at the time and still managin' the little shop downstairs. After Johnny died, I found I couldn't keep up the rooms in Mill Street, and so had given them up and was livin' with the bairns in the lodgin' house. Jack wouldn't stay there and so he stayed with his mother and the rest of his family in Woodbine Street.

Soon after, I had to give up the shop. There was always rats everywhere, but this shop was plagued with them and I was terrified for the sake of the kids. Ye hear some terrible tales about rats. But no matter what I did, I just couldn't get rid of them and they became so big and fat through eatin' my stocks, that their bellies were trailin' the ground. And so cheeky ye wouldn't believe it. They just sat there laughin' at ye. If I caught one, there would be two more to take its place. And when, one afternoon, a crowd watched two of them playin' in the window, bowlin' an egg before carryin' it out of sight, I knew the business was finished. By the time I'd settled everythin' with Mrs Prince, there was hardly a penny left.

I was now payin' Mrs Robinson twenty-one shillin's a week rent for the Thrift Street Lodgin' House. She had put it up from sixteen little by little each week since Mr Robinson died. And then she put it up for sale.

'How much do ye want for the ingoin', Mrs Robinson?' I asks her.

'Your money wouldn't buy it, Francie Nichol', was her answer.

Although me proper name was Francie Robinson, everybody called is Nichol. I don't know why, but they did. Maybe I wasn't a Robinson long enough for them to get used to it. Or maybe they just thought I wasn't good enough for the name.

A few days later she sold the place to two Arab brothers. In a fortnight one murdered the other and was hanged shortly after.

So all of us, Jack as well, moved to rooms in John Street. But after a few months he left the munitions factory. It was too hard work for the likes of him and he went away to look for another job. He was crafty and thought if he'd worked there he wouldn't be called up. And he wasn't, not till later.

I then went to live with Jack's mother in Woodbine Street. She treated is like a skivvy.

'You'd better pledge your sheets if you want a meal, Francie. The money doesn't come in on its own you know. And you've got to pay your way like anybody else in this family.'

I knew the market and all the market people very well. I had known them all me life since I was a kid hawkin' fish and greens. And again through Johnny. They had all followed Johnny's fights down there. Joe Hancock had been one of Johnny's best pals, and his father, old Mr Hancock, had long been a good friend. I bumped into him one day when I was down town, near the market place. He had a fish-and-chip shop and suggested that I take it. He had had all he wanted out of it, and was goin' to retire. I liked the idea. So did Mrs Callaghan. In no time she managed to raise a loan of £30 to buy the premises and fittin's. I was to work in the shop, while she was to see to the organisin', and the plan was to share the profits fifty-fifty between we. The business was to be in Mrs Callaghan's name since she had put up the money in the first place.

Shortly after, in October 1916, Edmund was born. He was a

proper little monkey and forever in a tantrum. And it was quite a job havin' to traipse all the way from Woodbine Street to the shop, back and forwards every day with the bairns. Mr Hancock was sorry for is and insisted on movin' into the downstairs flat behind the shop, and made me and the bairns take the upstairs one for free rent. It would save me time and effort, and give me the privacy he said I was entitled to. He knew that there was always rows goin' on at the Callaghans with their houseful of wild buggers, and he knew there was no love lost between me and Mrs Callaghan. She had been a schoolmistress one time, and had a superior air about her all the time. I was very grateful, but as it turned out I found meself with much more work to do. Mrs Callaghan quickly cashed in on the situation and made a convenience of is because I lived on top of the shop. I was havin' to open up, clean out, and get everythin' ready for the day's work. Everybody's greasy aprons were left for me to wash every night after the shop closed. I had to peel all the tateys, clean out the friers, prime them, and get them goin' again all by meself.

As well as all that, I did all the chippin' and fryin' without never as much as a kind word. And when she brought the fish in, I had to gut it and clean it. I was never allowed to take any money over the counter. All I got was me wages, but no fifty-fifty share of the takin's as we'd agreed. I got sick of it. Then Jack turned up. He still hadn't got heself a job. He was drinkin' like a fish and forever badly usin' is. Takin' his hands to is at the slightest excuse.

Edmund, the baby, had to be fastened into his bed and blocked in with barriers made from chairs and tables so that he couldn't get out and do heself an injury while I was workin' in the shop. The stairs were steep and he could have fallen down when I was in the back shop. And I would never know it. Mrs Callaghan didn't think that I was lookin' after her only grandson properly, and when her friend Mrs Barnett visited her, she would put me down and tell her what an awful neglectful mother I was to me bairns. I knew what was goin' on but seein' as she hadn't said anythin' to me directly, I just pretended it wasn't. But one day, she came right out with it in the shop.

92

Right in front of is. And was tellin' Mrs Barnett that I never cared a monkey's hoot for the bairns. But only for meself. And that I was selfish and vain.

So I said, 'Well, if that's the way ye feel, Mrs Callaghan, ye can stuff your shop and your business, and ye can go to hell. And ye can take your fish and chips with ye. And all fry together.'

I ran upstairs and cuddled me bairns tiv is as hard as I could.

'I love me bit bairns, I love all of yous. I'm only tryin' to do the best I can for yous. There, there, we'll get by.'

Just then, the door bursted open and Jack came flyin' in.

'I heard you, you bloody, cheeky bitch. Nobody talks to my mother like that. And least of all you! Take that! And that! And never open your foul mouth to her again. She's a better woman than you will ever be!'

Old Mr Hancock came runnin' up the stairs and pointed to Jack.

'I'm warning you, Mr O'Callaghan. If you badly use that lass once more, I'll get the police. You're always knocking her about. We are always hearing you, me and Mrs Hancock. But I'll tell you this. If you don't leave her alone, I'll have every policeman in town up these stairs and at you.'

Mr Hancock followed Jack down the stairs, leavin' me by meself with the bairns. He was a quiet, shy man and hated anything like this. It had obviously been too much for him, and he was near to tears. Ten minutes later there was a gentle tap on the door.

'Can I come in, Francie? It's only me, Mrs Barnett.'

'Yes, come in, Mrs Barnett. What's the matter?'

Mrs Barnett was a wealthy woman. Her family owned a chain of grocery stores. She was like a lady and had nice manners to go with it. She closed the door behind her, and looked all around the room, takin' it all in. Then she heaved a big sigh and said, 'Poor Francie. What a life you've got. What an awful, hard life. I'm really sorry for you and those little children. Can you not do any better than this?'

'You know I can't, Mrs Barnett. You probably know all about me already. What little there is to know.'

'Wouldn't you like your own business, Francie? I know you are a hard worker and get very little back for what you put in here. If you were working for yourself, you could probably do very well. Do you think you could manage the responsibility all on your own? With the children as well?'

'I once used to have me own little shop, Mrs Barnett. Well, nearly me own. That did fine. But it fell through what with one thing and another.'

'I can see you don't get on with Mrs Callaghan. She is a good friend of mine, Francie. And I wouldn't want to do anything to hurt her. But if you were to leave this place to Mrs Callaghan, and get your own business, Jack could work there with you. You would both be happy, and he wouldn't be so irritable as he is now, and . . .'

'But I haven't got two ha'pennies to rub against each other, Mrs Barnett. It's all very well to say get a place and. . . .'

'Now you listen to me, Francie. I'm going to lend you the money. But you mustn't say a word to a single soul, especially Mrs Callaghan. She must never know where the money has come from.'

'Oh thank you, Mrs Barnett, thank you. I'll pay every last penny of it back. Just as soon as ever I can.'

A couple of hours after, Mr Barnett came and said much the same thing as Mrs Barnett.

'Look around for a place that suits you, Francie. Take your time to find the right place, then snap it up. Whatever it is, we'll help you out. And see you all right, into the bargain.'

I told him how deeply grateful I was to them both and I promised to do as I was bid.

There was a run-down fish-and-chip shop on the corner of Gilbert Street and Frederick Street that I'd known about for some time. Just a gossip shop with very little trade. Far enough away, but handy all the same. And it had possibilities. Each night after I'd put the kids to bed, I'd slip out for an hour to watch the goin's on from across the street. At the time when business should have been at its best, it was dead. Hardly

94

anybody went in, and those who did stayed too long. I was carefully weighin' the situation up as I strolled past pretendin' not to look in the windows. But I was jottin' down notes 'n me mind all the time. A drunk in the corner and two women with their arms spread over the counter, chattin' away. Same thing night after night. No way to run a business that wasn't.

One night I went in to the shop about nine o'clock, and waited to be served. There were only two people waitin' in the queue but the owner who was servin' paid no attention to us at all. She was talkin' to Mrs Butler about Mrs Wilson's niece who was called Flora who was goin' with this queer feller from Hartlepool who had hurt his leg in the docks when he was unloadin' the sugar from that ship with the funny foreign name from Norway or Russia or some place like that and. . . .

Only three teeny little boilers. No proper pans or friers or anythin'. Tatey peelin's all over the floor. Two cats squabblin' over some fish in the back. No vinegar or pickles to be seen. The salt pot was dirty. The holes was closed up with grease, and it was empty into the bargain. The lino was worn away so ye could see the holes in the floorboards. Mice, almost certainly. Dead flies like blackberry jam in the little cracked window which was steamed up, and the fly-paper hangin' over the frier had too many flies on it. The counter was greasy and scruffy. Surely them walls weren't really yellow?

The old lady at the front of the queue got fed up and went out. I waited a bit longer then I asked for a ha'porth of chips. That was the smallest portion ye could get. 'Bring your own paper, Missus?'

'No.'

I took them outside, ate a couple, spat them out, and hoyed the rest away. They had too many black eyes and they were clay cold. They had been stewed so long in the fat they were all squelchy. And when you bit them they burst like peapods filled with drippin'.

'Good', I thought to meself, trade must be bad and she cannot expect much for that place.

I waited outside until she closed up, and then I tapped on the window.

95

I told her I had heard rumours that she wanted to sell up and that I was here to talk business.

'Forty pound the lot, Missus! It's a real thrivin' business and. . . .'

'Haad your horses, Missus. I'll take it. I'll be back tomorrow.'

The Barnetts were not only willin' to lend is the forty pound for the property, the stock and the goodwill, but also the extra sixty I reckoned I'd need to put in new counters, big windows, friers, condiments, and to do the place out and stock it. I was not sufficiently known to get tateys and fish on credit. Not yet, any road.

I knew there would be a hell of a row when the Callaghans found out. But as luck would have it, at least Jack was away again. Although I had threatened often enough to leave Mrs Callaghan's shop, I couldn't afford to, and she traded on it.

Every weekend, the Callaghans used to stay up at Woodbine Street and I would be left to me own from Saturday afternoon until Monday mornin'. So I arranged with some blokes from the market to move all me stuff downstairs and cart it away to Gilbert Street, before eight o'clock on the followin' Monday mornin'. When Mrs Callaghan came in with the fish she had brought from the market, the place was empty, and she went stark starin' mad. All that day she looked for is before somebody told her where I was.

'Where did you get the money from for all this?'

I thought she was goin' to burst a blood vessel.

'Sorry, Mrs Callaghan, but I've had quite enough. I told ye last week. You can do what ye like with your business. I've got mine, and it's my own. What I put into it, I get out of it. You'll see if I look after my bairns or not.'

Elbow grease. That was the way to succeed. That, with fair dealin's and cleanliness. Good service and a firm, strong hand. And all this was right up my street. So I buckled to and got things shipshape. I soon had them teemin' in and comin' back for more. I put out all the drunks and lingerers. Only good

96

tateys and fresh fish would I cook and sell. Tizer, pop and pickles. Beetroot, red cabbage and onions. Mussels and whelks. Fish-cuts ye could take out and cook yerself durin' the day. Batter, give them plenty batter. It cost nothin' and they loved it. 'Specially the kids. And it brought them back again and again.

'Can ye gis a bit batter, Missus?'

'Why aye, hinny. Will that do ye?'

'Grand. Ta, Missus.'

'Tell your ma, I'll have a nice bit of haddock comin' tomorrow. Lovely an' fresh. Don't forget, son!'

'Righto, Mrs O'Callaghan. Ta ta, Mrs O'Callaghan.'

'Ta ta, son.'

'Would ye like to take a jar of pickles wi' ye, Mr Jackson? They're really lovely. Just got them today. They're big 'uns as well, new ower from Gillies across the river. I've just had a couple, meself, and by, they're good. That's all right, ye can pay me tomorrow, hinny, when ye come for your chips. Hey Tommy, afore ye gan, why not take the missus a bottle of this? Lovely and sparkly it is. It'll wash that fish down nicely and help her digestion. Save her makin' a pot of tea, it will. She's been workin' all day and'll be tired. It's only threepence. . . . 'Course ye can. Here y'are. Ta.'

'Here, Mrs Charlton. For the cat. If ye come back tomorrow early, I should have a bit more. As long as I know you're comin', I can save somethin' for ye.'

Jack was keep comin' back, and goin' away again. Every time he came back there was trouble. Mr Barnett knew all about it. He had plenty influence and said he would drop a word in the right place, pointin' out that seein' Jack was no longer workin' in the munitions factory, he was available for callin' up. In a matter of days, Jack was called up to go and serve in the Army. It wouldn't do him any harm, all his brothers were doin' their share. I was glad. Now I could be left in peace to really get the business on its feet.

And so it went on from strength to strength. We lived sparin'ly. Nothin' extra for the shop and no improvements until

97

every penny of the £100 was paid back and I was cleared with the Barnetts. Once that was off me mind, I put the profits back in to buy all-around windows and new decorations. More friers I got, more chips, more fish, and a wide assortment of things to go with it.

Lizzie Flood came in to look after the bairns while I slaved away in the shop. Early in the mornin' I'd go out and buy fish, then come back and get the bairns ready for school. Then I'd clean and gut the fish and peel and chip the tateys. Then I'd clean and fry, and sell and fry, and sell and fry and sell. All day and till late at night. And I enjoyed mesel', I can tell ye, and God was good to me.

Fifteen shillin's a night was the takin's when I moved in. And now with chips at a penny a packet and fish at twopence, I was sometimes takin' nearly twenty pound a day. Ninety-five pound I was able to spend on a brand new set of friers. I was the first woman in South Shields to put up a queue rail to control the customers comin' in and keep some kind of order. Everythin', all expenses and everythin' were paid outright in hard cash. Two hundred pound saved in a bank account. A real bank account I'm talkin' about ye know, not just the post office. Like all the rich people have. With me very own name on the top. 'Missus Frances O'Callaghan.' Over and above that I had seventy-five pound in a little cloth bag hidden behind the mirror. And seventy-five pound is heavy. It felt grand when ye lifted it down, clinkin', to put more in.

I was now in a position to help me sisters and their families. I hadn't any time for visitin' or such like, but they used to come to the shop once or twice a week, and I never sent any of them away empty-handed. They were pretty unthankful though. I gave JaneAnne a job helpin' is with the weekly wash on a Monday mornin' for a few shillin's. And I always gave her some fresh fish to take away with her. Enough for her and Jim Kilcaldy and me father. I found out later that she used to go back and tell them I'd only given her the rotten fish I couldn't sell. Also, every week I'd send a hamper of food round with the bairns to make sure me father didn't starve. She didn't take any account of that, either.

10

As the years had went by and me father got older, he had got
softer. Everybody knew him as Old Nickler. And a bit of a
card. He was harmless now. Still a drinker, but only when he
was cute enough to get it. And still a bonny feller what with his
crop of white hair and rosy cheeks. He was a proper ladies'
man. I think he probably always had been. He had always
been quick to laugh at anythin' funny, and had a winnin' way
with him. He had little enough money but all of it was spent on
drink. He didn't believe in wastin' it on women. If they wanted
to earn his favours by buyin' him a drink, then that was all
right. But never the other way on.

I heard about his shinnanigens through Jim Kilcaldy who
used to follow him all over and spy on him. Kilcaldy would
earn his own drinks by tellin' tales about me father, in the bars,
goin' into all the gory details. Me father, who was much
craftier than Kilcaldy, knew all about the way he was carryin'
on, and he would invent all kinds of excuses to make him think
he wasn't up to anythin'. It was just like a cat and mouse game
they was always playin'. Wherever Old Nickler went, Kilcaldy
would be sure to follow and time and again he would jump out
at exactly the right moment and upset the applecart. Me father
had a good sense of humour but it must have been stretched to
the limits by Jim Kilcaldy.

On one occasion, he had gone a very roundabout way to try
to lose Kilcaldy and thought he'd done it for sure this time. He
was laughin' like a good 'un to heself as he was tellin' this lady
friend of his all about it and what kind of a fool Kilcaldy was.
Apparently he had been dartin' in one door of a pub and
straight out the other and losin' heself amongst the stalls in the
market-place. But he hadn't been quite quick enough this time,
'cos Kilcaldy had clung tiv'm like a leech. He kept out of sight
and bided his time. There me father's fancy woman was, laid
out on an old handcart with the wheels chocked up with two

half bricks. Her skirts were flung up around her shoulders and the old man's trousers were hangin' over the side. And there they were as brazen as could be, when Kilcaldy ran out from a doorway, grabbed the shafts and turned the cart over.

'That'll teach you to try to make a fool out of me, you dirty old bugger!'

Mind, Jim Kilcaldy had no real malice for me father. And it seems the old man bore him little in return. After all they had lived together in the same house ever since me father and I had parted in Foster Street, when JaneAnne had taken him in.

Wor JaneAnne and Jim Kilcaldy were among the very poorest of me relations. And this brought out the meanness in her. Every week I would send young Johnny and Joe over with three shillin's and sixpence for me father plus a few things to eat, in a little basket. He cared nothin' for the food, but was always anxious for the money to buy a drink with. He would wait for the kids to come on a Saturday with his allowance, and JaneAnne would try to waylay the boys and take the money off them. Whichever one got it first, would then deny black's white that they hadn't received it. This would always cause an argument. And I would get blamed for not havin' sent the money at all in the first place.

Me father used to take the wooden crates I'd give him from the fish shop, and chop them up into little bundles of firesticks. And then I'd sell them for him and give him the takin's. This was his only incomin's, and he worked hard at it all day and every day. Sometimes walkin' miles to collect scrap wood, bringin' it back, and makin' his bundles. His eyesight was gettin' so bad that I was worried for his fingers. Especially when his aim was off because of the drink in his head. Although by this time he couldn't read the money, he knew exactly how much he had by the feel of the coppers. And when, at the end of the day, he would put out his money on JaneAnne's table to pay for his board JaneAnne would quick as a flash sweep a shillin' under the tablecloth or through a knothole before he could count it. And then an argument would start, because he was no fool and had a pretty good idea how much he'd had before he came in. He didn't dare let them

100

know how blind he really was because he knew they would have the advantage on him. But they knew all the same, and they would challenge him to look for himself. And then he was beat. He knew it, and they knew it.

'I'm not bloody blind, you know! I can see how much there is.' But he couldn't really, not any more.

Whenever I saw me father in the street, I would always give him somethin' for a drink. Shirts and socks and vests that the boys had grown out of, would be washed, patched up and darned, and then sent round for me father. But he only finished up with what Jim Kilcaldy didn't want. Once, young Johnny won a huge pair of ex-army boots in a school raffle, and took them over to his grandfather. They were miles too big, but the old man was so proud of them, that he wore them all the time and everywhere. Every mornin' he would brush them hard to shine them up before goin' to seek his firewood.

One time when he took ill, I sent a basket of hard boiled eggs round to put him right. He'd ate one and was as sick as a dog. He told JaneAnne that Francie, his own daughter, was tryin' to poison him.

'She's the cheekiest little bugger I've got by far, and that's sayin' somethin'. I don't know why she's tryin' to do me in. I've got no money, so she's wastin' her time.'

Me bein' the youngest, he would always find fault with me first. I remember when I'd had the little shop in Thrift Street and Bob Charlton, Alice's husband, had come in and grabbed a hold of is. It hadn't been long after Johnny died. I had smacked him one and said that I remembered him of old, and that this time I was goin' to make him pay. I was goin' to tell wor Alice about him. Well, later in that same day, I'd got somebody to mind the shop and I was gettin' ready to go over to see Alice, when me father came in. He asked is where I was goin', and I told him. He says, 'Don't, Francie. They've got a lot of bairns. Think of wor Alice.' I was fastenin' me boots at the time and I stood up quickly to say somethin' to him, when me head smashed against his nose. It broke and there was blood everywhere. By the time I got him cleaned up, I'd forgot all about it and so I didn't go after all.

101

11

When the war ended, Jack O'Callaghan came home from the army to find heself in the money. He hadn't been farther than Kent so I'd seen him off and on. I'd got somebody to mind the shop a couple of times and had gone to his camp. He hadn't realised how well the shop was doin' and as soon as he got back and saw, he demanded to see all the account books and bank books and everythin'. Straight away. He nearly went crazy when he found out everythin' was in my name and not his. Him being away, I'd had to do it this way, but he said I had cheated him and done things on the sly. But I really hadn't. I only did things as I had thought for the best. For all of us and the bairns. He decided he wanted to buy some property. A place of our own that nobody could take away. He might of been right but I didn't think so, and I was the one who had sweated the blood. I told him I would make everythin' over in his name as well as mine if that would satisfised him. When we got to the bank he made such a fuss right in front of the clerks and everybody, with his arguin' and shoutin', that I said to him, 'You can keep the lot, Jack O'Callaghan. I'll sign all the money over to you to keep the peace, if that's what you want.' I felt awful. Those people liked me and I think they even respected is in a way even though I never made out I was anybody important. I've never done that to nobody. Let people find out and judge for theirsel's if you're worth takin' your hat off to.

So Jack now owned all the money and half of the business.

From then on he started, by God. If he wasn't worse for drink than me dad, he was every bit as bad. He couldn't get enough of the stuff. Day and night. He would go to the Buff's Club for a few beers first thing in the mornin' and then haddaway down to the fish quay. He used to buy the fish for me at that time, I will say that. But he would walk around

102

with a bottle of rum while he bargained. They used to call him the 'Rum King' down there. He used to even take Darkie the horse into the bar with him. Mind, Darkie was very well behaved, and he was so proud he would never eat anythin' in the street. It always had to be in the backyard. So I didn't bother me head too much about O'Callaghan. I just let him get on with it. As long as he let me and the bairns alone I didn't care what he did.

Little Francie had been born in December of that year, 1918, and Jack had sat downstairs drunk and singin' his head off while I was havin' her. He never needed no excuse to get drunk. He'd come back from the quay, drop the fish off at the shop and then go straight to the Buffaloes Club until teatime. He'd come back rollin' drunk and his tea had to be ready dead on time. Then a kip for an hour or so and out for another drinkin' session. I had to lay on at home for him nine bottles of beer and a bottle of red wine every single day that God sent. He always counted them as soon as he came in to make sure. I would be servin' in the shop and you could hear the click-clickin' and the pop-poppin' as the tops kept comin' off, with him swearin' at them all the while. It wasn't good for business, you know. People could hear full well and you could see them lookin' and wonderin' what was goin' on. And this sort of thing went on year in and year out, me doin' the workin' and worry-in' and him doin' the drinkin'.

And the bairns were growin' up.

12

1923. Johnny and Joe were such good pals, it did your heart good to see them together. They'd be about ten and eleven, and so different ye'd wonder what each saw in the other's company. Johnny was little and skinny and Joe was big and stocky. Johnny was the scholar and Joe was the dunce. Johnny was strict and strong-willed and Joe was soft as muck. Yet when it came to fightin', which they always did, there was

103

nothin' to choose between them. Although Joe was very strong and big, Johnny was lightinin' quick and tough and would never ever give in.

I wished they didn't have to be fightin' all the time. But that's the way God made them. And if I stopped them fightin' in the house, they'd only do it somewhere else. And if it had to be I'd rather them fight inside than outside. Because I knew that when they fought in the streets, some kids would be shoutin' for one and some for the other. 'Go on, give it to him, Joe!' 'Knock him out, Johnny!' Joe told me later on, that both he and Johnny hated the kids who were eggin' them on against each other and that often as not they turned on them durin' the fight and it would end up with him and Johnny on the same side. I do know that if either one of them was in any kind of trouble, ye'd see them walkin' up the lane with one of them havin' his arm on the other one's shoulder.

Although they never told me about their little bits of happenin's, I usually got to know about it all the same. Like one day, a lad from a higher class than Joe had swung him round in the yard and punched him. They had started scrappin' and a master had come out into the playground and told them that if they wanted to settle it, they must do it properly. He got a hold of two pairs of boxin' gloves and arranged the match for the afternoon playtime. The yard was packed with kids who wanted to see this big kid, who was a proper bully, in a fight with Joe Robinson. All the masters were there as well. The boys had took off their shirts and stripped to the waist in true style, and Joe knocked this other kid flat out in the first round. All the kids were yellin' and cheerin'. And from then on nobody tangled with wor Joe. Him and Johnny used to put on exhibition boxin' at the professional ring at Johnson's Hill when they were only eight and nine. They used to be called the Midget Wonders. Three rounds they'd do and people would chuck coppers into the ring. I never went but I was told the two of them were very popular and they'd always get cheered for their efforts. Ye just couldn't stop it. It was in their blood and it had to come out. Just like with their father.

Johnny was a very good scholar. Always I had school

104

reports sayin' how clever he was at this, that and the other. But wor Joe. . . . He was absolutely hopeless. He was hardly ever there, for what little good it did him. I used to march him to the gates and see him in, and afterwards I'd see Johnny picked him up at the gates. But God only knows where he'd been in the meantime. He always got in with the rough lot all his life. The hidin's he got at school never did him any good. But one day I found he'd been with a pinchin' gang. I lynched him and locked him in a dark cupboard for a few hours. He didn't do it no more after that. Even though he was wild and daft he would always be upset if he thought me or Johnny were really mad at him. Or disappointed with him. That would bring him to tears. But the next day he was the same again. He had a thick hide in some ways although he was dead soft in other ways. Johnny would always be havin' to get him out of scrapes. Their father would have been proud of them. Johnny and Joe. Joe and Johnny.

A terrible thing happened at this time that was to put paid to any ideas Johnny might have had of bein' a professional boxer. It all started when he was only seven. Mind I never knew the half of it. Not till much later on when it was too late to do anythin'. Johnny had just begun at his new school in Derby Street and he didn't know anybody yet. He'd been standin' in the playground when two kids started throwin' stones at him. Bein' so stubborn as he was, he wouldn't budge an inch. He just stood his ground till one of the stones hit him in the eye. He was cryin' when a teacher came up to him and said, 'What's the matter with you, bubblin' your head off like that? Don't be so bloody soft and get to your place before I clout your ear and really give you something to cry about.'

This had made Johnny feel very ashamed. And even though he couldn't see properly out of his right eye, he never told me. He hated anybody to think he was soft.

Nearly two years after that, he'd been gettin' the groceries in for is this day and was followin' a man smokin' a pipe up the stairs on a tram. This man had stopped halfway up and knocked his pipe on the rail to put it out, and the red-hot ash had teemed into Johnny's right eye. By the time he got home,

105

his eye was completely shut and was all red and swollen. I says to him, 'What ever's happened, Johnny! Have you been in another fight? What have ye done to your eye?' He told is about the tram, but only that. I bathed his eye in milk every day and the swellin' went down and the redness went away.

'It's all right, mother, it's getting better, I can feel it. It doesn't hurt as much as it did. Honestly.' After that, it really did seem to get better and he never said no more about it. So I stopped worryin' and forgot about it.

One night, two years later, when I'd been workin' in the fish shop, I'd had to go out into the yard for some more chips. As I passed by the lads' bedroom, I heard a quiet sobbin'. I opened the door very quietly and when I went in I found Johnny stiflin' his sobs into the pillow. I lit the lamp and held it up to his face. Ye couldn't see where his eye was. But where it should be, was like a lump of raw liver that was stickin' to the pillow-case. Awful stuff was comin' out. I did the best I could to comfort him and stop the pain. I crushed some quack tablets that usually worked for headaches in a glass of milk. The very next mornin' I took him to the Sunderland Eye Infirmary. They took him in straight away. After examinin' him they told is that Johnny's eye was so bad they'd have to operate immediately to save the other eye. A large abscess had built up behind the eye and was threatenin' his brain.

'If ye must, ye must. I can't do anythin' more for him. Yes, go ahead doctor. As long as I can see him first, before ye do it. I want to have a last look at him before it happens.'

But he said it would only upset him and I'd best go home and try not to think about it too much. Eleven years old, that's all he was. And to think it had been festerin' on for four years. And he'd kept it to heself all that time. I'd never realised until then what he'd been through. It was only when the infirmary doctor had been askin' him all these questions that it all came out about the months and months of awful headaches. How he'd been keep goin' blind. And how he'd used to keep seein' these blankets of blood in front of his eyes. Terrible things for a little bairn to suffer. And he never once moaned about it.

106

So I went home and bought a little dram of whiskey. I supped it and fell asleep.

Next day, I went back to the infirmary. Johnny was propped up in bed with his head covered in bandages. Only one little eye was peepin' out of all that tight white. As I was walkin' towards him I thought me heart was goin' to burst, but I didn't dare let it.

'Hello, son. Brought you this to eat. Made any pals, yet? Who's that poor little kid over there? Poor soul, he looks in a bad way.'

'Yes, he's had an accident, Ma.'

'Has he? Where? I bet he was up to somethin' he shouldn't have been doin'. Wor Joe's been away from school again so they tell me. The Board man's been round. You know, that truant master feller. He'll get such a hidin' tomorrow. I'll larrup'm when he comes home tonight. I'll murder him. . . . I'll. . . .'

'Ma, I've got a secret to tell you. It's going to upset you a bit, but it's not for you to worry. You see Ma they've taken my eye out.'

'Is that all you've got to tell me? That's nowt. You've still got one, haven't ye? Some people's got none. I know a lot with none at all. Nobody needs two when they've got one good 'un.'

Me own eyes were goin' to explode, I was sure.

Eventually, Johnny was ready to come home and I went to fetch him.

Sittin' beside him on the train, I wondered what I could say when I looked into that little face with no eye in it.

Suddenly Johnny said, 'Mother, have you ever seen the place where the eye should be when it's not there. Like the socket place I mean?'

'Your Ma's tough, I can look at anythin'. Nothin like that ever bothers me. Why like?'

'Well, you're never going to see mine, Ma.'

'Don't be daft. I'll have to bath it and all that, son. These drops have to go in. Ye cannot do it yersel'.'

107

'No, you won't. I'm always going to look after it myself. You're never going to see. Never!'

And I never ever did. Not to this day.

'I'm goin' to the chemists as soon as we get back, and I'm goin' to buy you the best glass eye that money can buy. One of the little thin ones that look nice. Just like the real thing. As good as a new eye it'll be, you'll see. Ye won't know the difference.'

Those sticky out ones they give ye are too thick. They bulge right out and stare at ye. And I didn't want one of them things for my little Johnny. He never cost is much for glass eyes because he used to take such care of them. He always kept his spare one in a little egg cup, locked away to heself. He was a funny lad, very careful. He broke the first one we got him, and he wouldn't go out. He said he was too ashamed. I said there was no call to be ashamed of a thing like that. It wasn't his fault. But I learned me lesson. Next time, I got him two. So he would always have a spare in case one got lost or anythin'.

13

In 1924 Walter was born and I had a bad time with him. He came out all blue. The midwife said it was caused by all the cold water I used to have me arms in when I was cleanin' and guttin' the fish for the shop. Whether it really was that or whether it was because he got strangled up while he was bein' born, I don't know. Just like when I'd had Edmund and Francie, O'Callaghan couldn't have cared less. I didn't even know where he was at the time of Walter, exceptin' that he'd been drinkin' in some place or another. Ye wouldn't get any prizes for guessin' that much. However, the Frederick Street fish shop was still goin' in spite of O'Callaghan and his antics. And so I wasn't complainin'. I'd long since got used to lookin' after meself.

One night, sometime in early 1925 it would be,

O'Callaghan was particularly bad with his sloppin' and swishin' and cursin'. I went into the back and told him to be quiet until the customers had gone 'cos it was bad for business. I made the excuse that I had come out for tateys. I was carryin' these in on a big basket, and as soon as I told him, he chucked a bottle of beer all over me face and hair and apron. Then he grabbed me arm and twisted it up me back. When he let go, I ran into the shop, took the fish-slice from the scaldin' fat, and ran back. Swish! Swash! Swoosh! into his face.

'Take that, ye sod! Take that'

I gave him a bit for the bairns as well.

I never had much time to spend with me bairns. I was always far too busy, but I loved them as much as any mother, all the same. When I was rushin' about here and there workin', I used to stop outside their bedroom door and listen to them talkin' or singin' to themselves. One night, I heard wor Joe cryin'—he was about thirteen at the time—and he was sayin' he was going' to run away the next day. And Johnny was tryin' to tell him not to.

I burst in and I says, 'What have I done that you would be runnin' away from is?'

'It's not you, Mother', Joe said. 'It's him. It's wor father. He's awful. He's always liftin' we up by wor lugs and hittin' we for nothin'. But don't tell him Ma, or he'll kill us.'

'I won't tell him, don't worry. Go to sleep and don't ever let me hear ye talkin' about runnin' away any more. I'll look after ye. No harm'll come to yous as long as I'm alive.'

So when I sloshed O'Callaghan with the fish slice, I remembered what the bairns had been sayin' the night I found them cryin'. I could see that he was stunned and I thought, 'Right, now's me chance.' Next, I grabbed the cinder shovel and smashed his legs with it. And by God, that fettled him. From that day on, he never quite knew how to take is, and he never forgot it. And every year after, for as long as I knew him, his legs would break out in sores. Just about the same time as well, like an anniversary. A kind of rough justice, you might say.

Not long before this had happened, a little old woman in the next lane who was very kind to the bairns, well, her man died.

She had nowt to look decent in even for her own man's funeral. They were only a little better off than paupers. She asked is if I could lend her a black coat and hat, which I did, naturally of course. O'Callaghan noticed it had gone and asked is where it was. So I told him. He said I had no right to lend our stuff out without his say-so. Had I hired it out? I said, 'No, course not. What d'ye take me for?' That was when he showed his mettle. He locked the door, put the key in his pocket and put my man's gloves on. He didn't even know how to wear them properly for all his brothers were fightin' men, real fightin' men. He hoyed a pair over to me and told is to put them on and squared up to is in his fashion. I was strong and I was tough, and I gave him back all I could. But he got is in the corner in the end, and bashed is till I was out for the count. I've never seen him in a fight with another man, mark you. In fact I've never seen him in a fight with anybody. Exceptin' me and the bairns that is.

Edmund, Jack's eldest bairn, was the one who was usually in trouble with his father. The lad was always goin' into tantrums and by God how O'Callaghan thrashed him. I had to go on me hands and knees to beg him to stop hittin' him. After Edmund had done somethin' one day, his father chased him into the yard. Edmund locked himself in the lav. O'Callaghan, after smashin' his fist on the door, hacked it down with an axe to get at him. I've never been a one for tellin' lies, but I had to to O'Callaghan. I know Edmund could be a bad little bugger when he wanted but he was only a bairn after all. If I was mad with him, I couldn't let O'Callaghan see for fear of what he'd do.

One time I thought he'd be had up. This Sunday was a special day for somethin' or other. All mornin' I had baked and baked to make a picnic. I never took the bairns anywhere 'cos I never had the time with the fish shop, but that day I'd made up me mind to take them to the beach. I dressed them all up and everythin' was hunkydory.

We got the tramcar down for a special treat. It was a lovely summer's day and the sun shinin' with all its might. As soon as we got there, Francie and Edmund wanted to go on the swings. So we all waited with the hamper and things until they'd had a few shots. But when the time came to go on to the beach, Edmund wouldn't budge off the roundabout. He yelled and he screamed till ye'd think he was bein' murdered and I pulled and dragged to get him off. But he was hangin' on to the pole as though his hands were stuck to it. People were lookin' and shoutin' and runnin' up and callin' is. Somebody fetched the police. I was past meself. They got Edmund off and took him down to the beach and threw salty water over him to try and shut him up. They brought back some water and chucked it over me as well. For me own good. I was so upset when I got meself put together again, that I grabbed hold of Francie and Edmund and ran all the way home with Johnny and Joe followin'. All the picnic things were left and we'd never even sat on the sands. Edmund was still yellin' when we came through the market-place. We bumped into O'Callaghan. He said, 'What the hell's goin' on? I thought you were supposed to be at the beach for the day?'

I was in such a state that I told him what had happened. He picked up Edmund and ran him all the way home. We had a big rain barrel in the yard and O'Callaghan ducked him till I thought he'd drown. But that cured him. I'm not sayin' O'Callaghan was right, but Edmund never again threw a canary fit.

But there was a time not long after that when Edmund ran wild, chasin' Joe and Johnny, with a knife in each hand. They couldn't control him or pacify him. It was as though he had gone clean out of his mind. Shoutin' at the top of his voice, jabbin' with the knives and laughin' all of the time. I took the knives off him, thrashed him, and threw him into bed. But no sooner had I left the room, than he was at it again. Downstairs in the fish shop the customers were waitin' to be served and were wonderin' what the hell was goin' on.

'I'll skin you alive, ye little sod!' I gave him another hidin' and clashed him on to the bed, but he just kept on laughin' and yellin'.

'I'll brain ye. Ye. . . !' I says, as I boxed his ears. Suddenly he vomited all over is.

111

'Blood! Oh, blood! I've damaged his little brain. Oh me little bairn, what have I done? What's your mother done to ye?' As I clasped him tightly to is, he struggled free and started laughin' all over again. I looked at him in sheer amazement. He'd gone completely crackers. Then he got up out of bed and ran to the cupboard and grabbed an empty bottle.

'Wine! Red wine! The little bugger's been drinkin' red wine. Here, gis a look! Oh my godfather! He's drunk the whole bloody lot. Your father'll murder ye when he comes back. You're drunk, ye stupid little fool. He'll kill us both when he comes in.'

Just then, Terry, O'Callaghan's sister, came in, and I told her all about it.

'There's no time to buy any more now, Francie. The pubs are all shut.'

'Can we fill it up with anythin' else that looks like wine?'

'It's no use, he'd soon know the difference. You'll just have to tell him the truth, Francie'.

As we were talkin', in came O'Callaghan who went straight to the cupboard.

'There's a serious thing happened here tonight, Jack. That little bairn, your own bairn, has been drinkin' your wine.'

O'Callaghan looked at Edmund who was very white, very sick, and in an awful state. He turned to his sister and said, 'That's it, Terry. That's the finish. I never bring another drop into this house as long as I live.' With that he went to bed and said no more. What a relief. But needless to say, the cupboard was stocked up again same as ever the next day.

All the while O'Callaghan was spoilin' the business and by 1926 it was goin' down and down. Folks would come in for a few fish scraps and he would knock them out me hand and chuck them in the fire. 'What do you think this is? We sell fish here! We don't give it away! If you buy it, you can have it. If you don't, that's where it goes.'

He'd come in drunk and want me to go to bed with him straight away. Before nine o'clock even he would stagger in and rake all the fires out and we had to close up. That's the best time in the fish-and-chip business, when folks are comin' late from work or out the pub. I would still be servin' and he'd slam the frier lids down and say, 'That's enough! Finished for the night. You can all beat it till tomorrow.'

He would turn anybody away who couldn't pay there and then. And he once hit is in the shop just because I gave some kids some batter for nowt. I told him not to worry, I would give them a few chips less to keep the weight right. But he knew I wouldn't. I couldn't do a thing like that, it was so mean. They got charged for everythin' down to the last bit of cracklin' when he was there. He'd have sold them the fins off the fish's backs if they'd asked for them. He'd come out of the pub and grab is in the shop, in front of everybody, and shout, 'Howay to bed, Francie!' I used to smile and pretend that he was just actin' daft-like, but I could have turned blue with shame. He was a very lustful man. Just like a stallion he was.

Me niece Gertie, wor Lily's girl, was livin' with us then. We'd taken her because Lily was very hard up at the time, and we fed and clothed her in return for her helpin' out in the shop and lookin' after the bairns. She liked it with us and O'Callaghan put up with it for the sake of the business. She was just turned fifteen, a lovely girl she was, and very well built if you know what I mean. Very big titties for her age and like a grown woman round the hips. She was such a quiet lass with a really nice nature.

Well, this day I had been cleanin' the fish out in the yard, and I heard her shout. 'Auntie! Auntie!' Just twice like that. But in a queer sort of voice.

I wiped me hands on me apron and ran across the yard to the bottom of the stairs.

'Are ye all right, Gertie? Gertie, was that you?'

'Yes, Auntie. But I'm all right. Don't worry.'

Three weeks to the day, the same thing happened. I ran across the yard and up the stairs in me fish clogs and found Gertie all white and shocked lookin' and draped on the stairs.

'Whatever's the matter with ye, pet? Come on, tell me quickly. What is it?'

She could hardly get the words out. 'It's me Uncle Jack, again.'

113

'What about your Uncle Jack? What about him, Gertie? Come on now, don't be frightened. Tell me. Nobody's goin' to hurt ye.'

Gertie had apparently been scrubbin' the stairs and O'Callaghan had crept up behind her and put his hand up her skirt.

'Oh, me little bairn. I knew he was . . . but I never thought he'd stoop so low as to do a thing like that to a little girl. You wait here hinny, I'll soon fix him.'

I ran down the back stairs the way he'd went, as fast as me legs would carry is, and I ran hell for leather down the main street, clogs and all. I still had me fish apron on and scales all over me hands. I knew where I'd find him. And there he was sure enough, in the Buffaloes Club with his cronies, sittin' round a big iron table drinkin' beer. I started on him, and his mates just laughed. They must have thought the randy swine was a real champion.

'You bloody child raper, you! I'm workin' in the yard right next to ye practically, and ye would sneak up behind me back and do a thing like that to a little bairn. Ye should be ashamed of yerself, Jack O'Callaghan.'

I got hold of the table by the legs and threw it over. All their beer spilt on the floor. Then I came out. I went back home half expectin' him to come after is and murder is in the street. But he didn't. He didn't come home until late that night. And when he did eventually come, he just went to bed and said never a word about it. I thought he must have learned his lesson and realised the very bad thing he had done.

If our Lily had known she would never have spoken to me again for lettin' that happen to her daughter. After the bother, I had told Gertie she had better go home as it would be for the best. But she wouldn't. She said she knew what I was thinkin' and she would never ever tell nobody about it. She said she loved me so much she didn't know whether she loved her own mother or me the best. She was a canny bairn, a lovely nature.

However, O'Callaghan did not give up by any means. If anythin' he got bolder, once grabbin' her while I was at church havin' little Walter christened. I decided to try a different tack

114

with him. He would take no notice of my pleadin's or scoldin's and obviously he had no consideration at all for the tender feelin's or years of Gertie, so I called in the priest. He was little more than a lad and it turned out to be a big mistake. He told is I was exaggeratin' it all, that I'd promised O'Callaghan love, loyalty and obedience at the altar and that I must abide by those promises. He said I should go to Mass every mornin' with the bairns and ask for Our Lady's help. He even said I should be extra nice to me husband, give him a treat for his supper like a slice of gammon or a pair of kippers. As if that would count for anythin' with him. 'But what about him, Father? Aren't ye goin' to say anythin' to O'Callaghan? Are ye goin' to let him get away with it, scot-free?'

'Look, now Frances, "Love and Obey". And don't forget the parable, "Let him who is without stain of sin cast the first stone." Are you without that stain of sin, Frances? Eh? No, I'm sure you're not. You will have to come to confession at least once a week without looking for idle excuses. It's only a very little time out of your week.'

'You have the damned nerve to tell me, Father. . . . To tell me all that about goin' to church and confession and every-thin', and yet ye let that randy sod get away with it. . . . I'm sorry, Father. . . . I didn't mean to say that. But that's what I think, and I have to say it. . . . Serve and obey that womaniser? Not on your life. I don't want no more of you and your talk. You're as bad as he is, almost. Get out of my house and never come back no more! I don't need you.'

Many years after that when I went back to the Church, I was very sorry for what I'd said to the priest because I know ye could go to hell for talkin' to a Father the way I had done. But it wasn't for a long long time. Anyway the priest had evidently said nowt at all to O'Callaghan because he got worse than ever.

One afternoon, I was takin' the baby to see his Grandma Callaghan. 'I won't go up to see me mother today, Francie. I was round there just last night. You go up with the kids and call for me at the club on the way back, and I'll come home with you.'

115

So, after visitin' Mrs Callaghan, I waited outside O'Callaghan's club for closin' time. I didn't dare go in. Half an hour passed by. The club had emptied, the windows were shuttered. I thought I must have missed him and so I went home. Maybe he had forgot the plans and had gone home sooner on. Or what was more than likely, he had gone to a different pub.

When I got back home, it was pitch black. Not a light on and everythin' locked up. Even the back-door. I felt that somethin' was wrong. I wrapped little Walter up in me coat and put him in a tatey box in the washhouse, and then I crawled through the coalhouse hatch and up the stairs into the house. And there he was. . . . He'd been clartin' on with that bairn again. She was sobbin' her heart out on the bed and he was lyin' there with his arms folded behind his head, with his muffler on. I grabbed the ends and pulled them around the bedhead. I would have surely choked him to death once and for all but he woke up just as I thought I had him.

Next day I marched up to Mrs Callaghan's and spilt all the beans out. I told her about the business with Gertie, about the priest, everythin'. I held nothin' back. Ye could see Mrs Callaghan was really shook up and didn't know how to tackle it. She was a crafty old woman though, and a good mother. Strict Catholic she was and very loyal to her sons, no matter what they did.

'It's your fault, Francie. He is only a normal healthy man with normal healthy appetites. What can you expect if you don't satisfy him? He's as good looking as any young man you'll find, and you're lucky to have him. Where would you be without him to help you bring up all those children? You need a husband and they need a father. They are his bairns as well you know. Don't forget that. And you couldn't have managed without him getting the fish in for you. It's a hard and thankless task going out every morning, come hail or shine, arguing and bandying down there. And then having to hump cold and slimy fish all the way back. What man worth his salt doesn't have a drink after that? Just because you don't like a drink, doesn't mean that he shouldn't, does it? I think you're a bit selfish you know, Francie. You should stick by him, not be always running him down like you do.'

'I can't be peelin' tatties, cleanin' fish, lookin' after five bairns, fryin' and servin' in the shop, and be upstairs lyin' under him at the same time. And it's late and I'm dead beat by the time I've finished. And if I cannot give him what he wants when he wants it, he rips me nighties to shreds and chases me out into the street at dead of night.'

'Now just be careful what you say, Francie. Watch your language with me, my girl. I'm no fishwife. My background and upbringing was a lot different to that. Don't be vulgar, or. . . .'

'Look, Mrs Callaghan, I've heard enough. All right, so that's the way it is. I can see I'm gettin' nowhere talkin' to you. I thought you might have understood and helped. Well, right. I'm goin' straight from here to the solicitor's. I'm goin' to have him up. I'll get the police on him. That'll soon put a stop to his shinnanigens.'

Now, I know she was me mother-in-law and older than me, and a grand talker and all that, but I had heard enough. I'd listened to her speak her piece but I wanted no more of it. She knew I was in a bad temper and she knew I was tough enough to do what I said I would do. So she took a different tack, speakin' quieter and pleadin' with is now. She said I must think about the bairns and what a court case would do to them. They might get taken off is, even. And she would speak to Jack herself. He would listen to her and take notice of what she said. So, I said all right and that we'd leave it at that.

But in less than a week, O'Callaghan was at it again. And so I had no other choice but to send Gertie back home to Hull. Fortunately, Lily and her man had bought a fish-and-chip shop themselves in Hull and had written to me askin' if I could spare Gertie. She would be very handy to them as she knew a good bit about the fish-and-chip shop business by now and would be able to tell them all they wanted to know. And they would only have to give her her keep and not worry too much about wages. When I told her that I'd decided she should go, she begged is to let her stay.

117

I told her that it was for her own good and showed her the letter from her mother and father askin' is to let her go. And so she went, and we were all sorry.

Down and down went the fish-and-chip shop. Then I found meself landed with repayment for a loan of £50 that O'Callaghan had taken out for his mother. Why, I don't know. But he did. He hadn't breathed a word to me about it. And the first I knew was when this feller came round from the money-lender's askin' for the first instalment. Apparently O'Callaghan had mortgaged everythin' in the shop down to me last pan. By this time I couldn't get anybody to help is in the shop because they couldn't abide O'Callaghan.

As soon as there was enough money in the till to buy a glass of beer, O'Callaghan would be away out. I'd leave enough of the takin's in the till for him to get a couple of beers, and hide the rest. Otherwise he'd have taken the whole lot. He used to sit heself near the window in the bar across the road, so he could see how many customers would be comin' into the shop. This way he could work out how much money was comin' in. He was nobody's fool, drunk or sober. He'd wait till I'd closed up and drawn the blinds, and then he'd come in. He'd grab is by the hair and fling is into the yard. Then he would punch and kick is until I was sick. It was for certain that we'd have no business left at all at this rate. Even he realised that. And that meant that soon there'd be nowt for him to drink with. That was all he cared about. He didn't give a tuppenny damn about me and the bairns. A small fish-and-chip shop came up for rent in Edith Street and I talked him into takin' it for heself. I would look after the Frederick Street business and that would be our keep. He could have the Edith Street and what profit he made there he could have just for drinkin'. This suited him so we went ahead.

With him out of the way, the Frederick Street business picked up again. Which was just as well because in a couple of months his shop in Edith Street was completely snookered. So we had to get rid of that. We tried again with a new shop in

Walpole Street but it wasn't long before that was goin' downhill too. Only a matter of weeks that was.

14

Johnny had been goin' to St Bede's grammar school and doin' very well. I was really proud of him. He left when he was fifteen, but things were hard and he couldn't get a job anywhere even though he was dead keen. So he went and fixed up to go to sea with his uncle Jim Callaghan who was a ship's cook. I did everythin' I could to persuade him against it. But there was no budgin' him. He'd made up his own mind and set his heart on it. I knew he was doin' it for my sake so's he wouldn't be a burden to is. And I also knew he wanted a bit of adventure. After all he was growin' into a man, and he hadn't had much of a life up till now. It would broaden his mind. And maybe it would make him sprout away. Because even though he was a strong and tough little feller, he was still very small. So ... away he went. His little bright face was full of smiles. I'd had only a couple of days to get him ready and to fit him out with the things he needed. White aprons, and long trousers and things like that. He had to join the ship at Hull, so I made him wear his school cap and shorts to get there for half price.

A couple of days later the ship was comin' back to Shields to pick up its cargo and so we all went down to see Johnny. It was a Sunday afternoon and all the bairns were standin' on the Groyne to see him off. He wasn't allowed to leave the ship of course so we were shoutin' across to him. Although he was glad we were there, he was pretendin' that he hadn't seen we, so's none of the crew would think he was soft. He had his apron on and his long trousers and was pullin' on this great big rope with all these big sailors. Poor little soul. I couldn't help meself from shoutin', 'Come back son! Don't go. Come on home!' But he didn't hear is. Or at least he didn't seem to. When the ship shoved off we stood and waved till he was long out of sight. We

119

watched until it was just a little speck on the ocean. And I thought to meself, 'There he goes, my little Johnny. Gone away to foreign lands, all by heself.' I couldn't help cryin' as we all humped back home.

Three months after, he was back. And there was such a change in him. Bigger and older. At least I thought he was. He'd brought back a little metal box called a ditty box and it was full of coppers that the other seamen had put in for him. He had been very popular with them all. They wanted him to sign on for another voyage but this time I said no. I needed him at home with me. I needed his brains and his backin'. And although he'd have gladly gone away again given half the chance, I think he was contented at least that he'd seen a bit of the world.

Straight away off he goes and gets heself a job on the roads, makin' the navvies' tea. Whilst he was there he was writin' letters for jobs all over the place. I wish I could have written letters like that. All neat and clever and no spellin' mistakes. Anyway, this mornin' a letter came through the door addressed to Mr John Robinson. I ran out and caught the postman and I says, 'Here, there's no John Robinson lives here.' So he took it back. Just then there's a shout behind is and up comes little Johnny. 'That's me, Ma. That's me,' he says. 'I'm Mr John Robinson.'

'You, Johnny?' I says, 'You? Yes, I suppose ye are. Why of course ye are, son.'

So I fetched back the letter off the postman and Johnny opened it up. It was from the Guardians. They were offerin' him a fortnight's work writin' out food vouchers for the Strike. Ten bob each they were worth. This was a really important job. My little Johnny sendin' these letters to people all over, tellin' them how much money they could have. Well, when the fortnight was up, the boss calls him into the office and says, 'Well Johnny, your fortnight's up. You understand that the job was only for two weeks, don't you?'

'Yes, gentlemen, I do,' he says. 'And I wish to thank you very much.'

'You thank us very much, Johnny? No, it's we who should

120

thank you. And what is more, we are not going to sack you, because we couldn't do without you. We are keeping you on, and you can work for us as long as you're willing to.'

So what about that, eh? Good lad, Johnny.

Joe also left school in 1927 and he got a job as a joiner's apprentice at Redheads in the shipyards. Of course he was always actin' the daft lad and soon got heself into trouble. This day the apprentices had been messin' about with a fire extinguisher and broke the end off. Once the stuff started squirtin' out they couldn't stop it. The foreman came on the scene so wor Joe clasped it to his belly and jumped into a bin with it. It shot out the top, the bin rolled over and he fell out sprayin' the foreman and heself so they both had to go home and get changed into dry clothes. So when they closed down shortly after because of the strikes and all that, wor Joe was the first to be given his cards.

Young Edmund who was now nearly twelve was workin' as an errand boy at a greengrocer's. One day the boss came to tell me that Edmund had pinched a few shillin's. He called it a mistake. But it was pinchin' as far as I was concerned. Downright stealin'. I offered him the money but he wouldn't take it. I was really upset, and when O'Callaghan came in he soon found out all about it. Later on he'd seen Edmund in the street and told him that when he got home he was goin' to skin him alive. When I got back from work, I found a message from Edmund. It said, 'Dear Mam, by the time you get this, I'll be out of existence.'

I didn't pay too much attention 'cos I knew what he was. He would deliberately play on your feelin's. But as soon as wor Johnny came back from work, I sent him to look for Edmund. It was the next day before he found him and when he brought him back he was stinkin' of turnips and horse's muck. Apparently he'd slept out in this farmer's field all night. By this time I'd got very worried and had taken his picture to the police. He was so sorry-lookin' for heself that I told O'Callaghan he'd learned his lesson and that I'd thrashed him, so to let things be and forget it. Which he did, thank God.

Up the road a bit, was the Thompsons. What a funny bunch

121

they were. The father was a coal merchant and he used to have the biggest horses you've ever seen. Hackin' great things they were. Like elephants. He had this horsewhip which he laid more often across the backs of his sons than he ever did across his horses. He didn't half make them trot along. To see them on the move, you'd think they were Derby winners rather than poor old cart-horses pullin' sacks of coal. I've never seen a stricter man on his bairns. Mind they deserved it. They were a wild bunch. That's why wor Joe used to knock round with them.

Old Mr Thompson would have these kids at church on a Sunday mornin', all dressed up with straw bengers and everythin'. He'd sit on the corner of the street with the smell of the Sunday dinner waftin' around, in his longjohns with his whip across his knees. As soon as the boys got back from church, he'd have them all changed in their old clothes and runnin' around like they'd come straight out of hell rather than church. Mind he was crackers heself so ye couldn't expect the kids to be any better. One thing he hated, and everybody roundabout knew it, was washin' on a line. People used to string their clotheslines right across the backlanes from wall to wall. And him bein' a coalman, he had to go up the lanes. He'd stand straight up on his cart at the bottom of the lane and shout, 'Shift your bloody washin!' Then, without givin' anybody a chance, he'd gallop up the lane and dozens of lines would be dragged to the ground and covered with coal dust. One such mornin', one of his lads had wanted to have a game of cricket with wor Joe. The father had given him a good cloutin' and told him to get on with his job. Well, as the old man was gallopin' up the lane, his lad was lookin' over his shoulder at wor Joe standin' with his cricket bat. 'Watch out, ye stupid little bugger!' the old man shouts to his lad. But as he turned round to his father, one of the lines caught him by the throat and he was left danglin' there like he'd been hanged. That was Mr Thompson.

By the end of 1927 I had to give up the Frederick Street shop. I couldn't keep both that and the Walpole Street shop goin', so I sold that business and concentrated all me energies

122

on Walpole Street. We were livin' there now so I couldn't afford to let that one go.

We struggled on and on until 1929 and then that went the same road. O'Callaghan laid that one out in the same way ne done the others. And that was the end of that. No more fish-and-chip shop businesses for me. We now hadn't a single penny to wor names. We had to move out and look for somewhere else to live. We had absolutely nowt. And still I had O'Callaghan. Like a useless millstone round me neck.

I was forty now. I had old bairns and I had young bairns. But they were still all just bairns that had to be looked after. I still had a responsibility to me sisters and to me father. And, I'm sorry to say, to me husband, Jack O'Callaghan.

15

After searchin' and searchin' and draggin' the bairns around everywhere with is, I found a house with cheap rent in Hudson Street, and we all moved in. It was only goin' to cost us thirteen shillin's a week. Next thing was, I got a job scrubbin' out Campbell's common lodgin' house in Tyne Dock, and Mr Barnett found O'Callaghan a labourin' job.

'The man's no good, Francie, but at least it'll keep him off your back a bit.'

At first O'Callaghan was givin' is a pound a week.

'Surely to God you're gettin' more than this? There's seven of us to feed you know, Jack.'

Then he threw up his job because of a bad back, and we were now worse off than ever. Joe hadn't got a job at all, and Johnny was only bringin' in seven and six a week and that didn't go very far.

One day I had fourpence and that was all I had in the world, and I was at me wits' end. I'm not a gambler and I had never used a slot machine in my life, but I saw this machine and thought to meself, 'Kill or cure, I've nowt to lose.' I put it in penny by penny determined to lose the lot or make me fortune. Twelve and odds came shootin' out. Dang, clatter, bang bang! I thought all me Christmases had come at once. I bought some groceries and two bob's worth of coal to cook the grub properly. By, that was grand. A real godsend from heaven.

I had been addin' to me wages at the lodgin' house by doin' paintin' and decoratin' for an extra few shillin's. Ye could always get ceilin's to do. They were so high and so dirty that real painters would have nowt to do with them. Not so, me. I used to wash down walls ready for the painters, but the ceilin's I would wash and paint meself.

Mr Campbell allowed is to do this work as a bonus. With five bairns and an idle man to support, he knew the wage he was payin' wouldn't go far enough. He knew I had a lot of debts to pay because I was always askin' for extra work. Could I cook for the lodgers? Would I do some laundry? Could I do a bit of this and help with that?

One night, after doin' the lodgin' house ceilin's, I had a terrible attack of lumbago. When I came home I could not sit or stand and if I lay down, every time I moved, pains shot through is like daggers.

'You'll have to help is with the bairns tonight, Jack. I feel as though somebody's twistin' gulleys in me back, all over.'

'It's no use you complaining. I'm laid off work with my back. It's far worse than yours, caused by taking on too much hard work. Outside in all weather. Lifting and shovelling. I've been trying to do the work of two men to get money to pay for you lot. My back's broken under the strain. I've probably cracked my spine. Not that that would matter to you, with your little bit aches. A touch of rheumatism that's all you've got. But you have to make such a song and dance about it. If I don't get right, I'll never be able to work again. We can't rely on you. You're always having kids. And look at the money you get. It wouldn't keep a canary. So shut your gob, and leave me alone.'

By now I hated O'Callaghan so much that, God forgive me, I tried to poison him. Mr Campbell used to have some weedkiller that he used to finish his dog off with because it was gettin' to be a nuisance. I thought to meself, 'If that stuff's good enough to do in a big, strong dog like that, it should be the very thing I'm lookin' for for O'Callaghan.' So I brought some home and I sprinkled it all over his dinner. He didn't come in till very late that night and I kept heatin' it up and then it'd get cold, and I'd heat it up again. I was determined not to waste that poison. At last he came in and sat down at the table. I had put the kids to bed very early on because I didn't want them to see what was goin' to happen. I got out his dinner and set the table nicely with salt and vinegar and pepper. He took one look at it and he says, 'What the hell's that?' I says, 'What the hell does it look like? It's your dinner, isn't it? If ye'd come in at a proper time, it'd 've been fit to eat. I'm makin' no more so you'd better just get on with it.' He got up, took the plate, clashed the lot in the fireplace and went out. I went upstairs and fell on me knees to thank God. And I never ever tried anythin' like that again.

An anonymous letter was sent to Mr Campbell printed in big block letters accusin' him of me bein' his mistress. He was ravin' mad because it dirtied his good name. He showed it to me and I didn't know what to say. I was beside meself with shame.

'I've no idea who it could be, Mr Campbell. Honestly I haven't. I don't know whose writin' that is.'

I had my suspicions though, and so did Mr Campbell. But I wouldn't dare say mine because he swore he would find out and take the slanderer to court and break them. All that happened was that he said it would be for the best if I didn't work there any more so that it would give nobody any cause to point their finger at him.

I think he felt sorry for is so he tried to help is to get another place.

'I have a bit of property in Leighton Street that would suit you fine, Francie. It has six rooms, stables, outbuildings, and is in very good condition. It wants doing up a bit, but you could have it nice and fit to live in in no time. It would make a lovely home for you all. The kids would have plenty room to play and

125

Jack would just have to keep a job down once you got there. It's ideal for you. What about it, Francie?'

'But I've got no money, Mr Campbell. We're broke. Where would I get all the money to buy a great big house like that? It's out of the question.'

'Look, it's perfectly sound. You'd get a full mortgage on it. It wouldn't cost you much, paying in small instalments. The land's big enough to build a public house on if you wanted.'

'Oh, Mr Campbell. D'ye think we're made of money? It doesn't grow on trees you know.'

'All you would have to find, is the money for the solicitor's fees and they won't be much. You can take your time to pay them. They're never in too much of a hurry to press their bills. Not in cases like yours.'

'Well, thank ye very much, Mr Campbell. I'll think about it. I'll talk it over with O'Callaghan.'

'Look Jack, we must put our brains in steep over this, and see what we can come up with. Now that wor Johnny's started workin' he's bringin' in seven and six a week, regular. You're gettin' a quid or so on the buildin's now, and if I asked Mr Campbell if I could stay on, there's twenty five bob a week for a start.' I'd heard that Mr Campbell couldn't get anybody else to take my place and that he wanted is back again. It would be our own property and that was what O'Callaghan had always wanted.

But the day we moved into Leighton Street, O'Callaghan gave up his job. Joe was away at sea, and even though it was costin' nothin' to keep him, there was nothin' comin' in from him neither.

Wor little Johnny was a hard worker though. He was honest, respectful and well liked at the office where he worked. And he was willin' to work any amount of overtime to get a few extra coppers for his mother. He once came in with three pound bonus money. I'd bought O'Callaghan a new suit with it and some hens to occupy his mind. What with those and the little money that I could spare for his drink, he wouldn't bother us so much. And we'd be left free to get on with things. Every egg he gave is, I paid for. But he charged no more than anybody else so I had to be satisfied with that.

Johnny's wages was enough to pay for the mortgage payments and I always put that aside for that very purpose. Every Friday, before settin' out for the lodgin' house, I would divide up the money in portions. So much in the pewter for the gas bill, so much under the clock for the coal, so much here for this and so much there for that, for when the collectors came. The mortgage had to be paid at the big office down town and this was O'Callaghan's responsibility. Everythin' was goin' well and I couldn't have asked for more.

One night, after a particular wearyin' day at the lodgin' house, I came home. I'd had an awful job gettin' Walter off to school that mornin'. He had kicked up such a fuss. I hadn't heard from wor Joe for a long time and he had gone a long way this time. Little Francie had the measles and was in bed cryin' when I had left to go to work. Johnny was lookin' a bit peekish about the gills these days. He was takin' on far too much book readin' for one so young. They'd got him on studyin' about the laws for the poor people. Poor kid couldn't study properly at home. There was always too much noise. Me neck was stiff and me back ached. It had been the day for scrubbin' the big yard and me knees were full of grit. What a mess I looked. I had carried a headache round with is all day after O'Callaghan had boxed me ears the night before. It was very windy and the garden was full of papers and rubbish that had blown in.

'I wish he'd do somethin' about that gate. . . . I wonder if little Francie is any better?'

When I opened the door, there was a great big pile of demandin' letters all over the floor. All bills. Gas was three months overdue, and they were threatenin' to close it off. Coal, unpaid for a month, and no more deliveries to be made until all bills were paid in full. The grocer was takin' legal action. Another gas bill, and another. And here is one sayin' they are comin' to shut it off on Thursday. Thursday? That's tomorrow. And the best of the lot was four letters from the buildin' society. They were goin' to take the house off us. After two

127

whole years of effort gettin' it put right, just the way we wanted it.

'Oh my God. . . . What's the meanin' of this, Jack?'

'You've read them, haven't you? You can see as well as me. What are you going to do about it? Sue them all?'

'For how long has this been goin' on? Just tell me that will ye?'

'Don't ask me. I saved them all up for you so you could deal with them all at once. It's easier that way. And don't start blaming me and shouting with your foul mouth, you fuckin' bitch, or I'll bash your stupid bloody brains out.'

'I've never asked ye once all this time because I trusted ye. Trusted ye with all our hard-earned money. I never thought ye were this bad.'

'Shut up! I've warned you, I won't tell you again!'

'Well, I'm goin' straight out now to find out if all this is true. And if it is, and they're really goin' to do all these things to us, I'm leavin' ye. Once and for all.'

I only had to make two calls to find out that everythin' was true. There was no point traipsin' round them all and gettin' meself embarrassed. It would only be a waste of time. I collected up all the bills and put them in me purse. They would all be paid in due course.

'This time I'm really goin', O'Callaghan. And I'm takin' the bairns with me. All of them. I mean it this time. I'll leave you the house and everythin' in it. I want nowt. You keep it and see what you can make of it. Here, you'll need that. Sort that lot out on your own.'

I tossed him all the letters to do with the house and property. 'I won't be needin' that any more.'

'Go on then. Get goin'! I couldn't care less.'

I flopped meself down in the chair and O'Callaghan went out.

I heard this whistlin' and Johnny came in.

'Whatever's the matter with you, Ma? I've never seen you so upset-looking.'

I gripped Johnny's little white hand in my big red one.

'I'm goin' to look for another place for we, Johnny. Will you

128

come with is, son? I don't know what I'd do without you. I've got to do it now while the iron's hot, or tomorrow I'll forgive him and we'll be back where we started. I want to go now before I calm down or I'll never do it.'

' 'Course I will, Mother. Come on. Where shall we look first?'

'Let's go and see your cousin Harry in Ford Street. His wife's in the estate business. He might know of somethin'.'

The only thing on the books was a two-roomed place at the back of the Robin Hood in Primrose. And that was not up to much accordin' to Harry Robinson.

'We'll take it. I don't care what it's like. I don't even want to see it. When can we move in? Tonight. . . ? Right. Thank ye very much, Harry. You're a good lad. Need we not pay in advance, till the end of the week? Till me money comes in? I've got a good job and I'll be able to pay all right. It's just that I'm a bit short at the moment.'

These two rooms were small and they were scruffy. There was nothin' on the floor and nothin' on the walls. Even the plaster was peelin' off. Loose boards and mouse holes was all over. Great gaps round the windows. The spuggies (sparrows) used to come in and fly around. Mind, I didn't mind those poor little things. They can't do ye no harm even if they are as bold as brass. They're better than beetles. The wind and rain always came in, ye just couldn't keep them out.

The ramshacklin' tin-pot beds were overloaded with bairns, and were always collapsin' durin' the night. Me and Johnny would get up to sort out the bairns from the blankets and try to put them all back in some kind of order. I was terrified in case it would happen one night without is hearin' and that me bairns would all be suffocated.

On the way to work, I used to walk along the road hopin' to hitch a lift from the lorries into Tyne Dock. Sometimes I got one but most often I didn't, and then I would walk all the way there and back. All in all it would be about twelve miles, because after I had cleaned out Mr Campbell's Tyne Dock lodgin' house, I did five others with one in Thrift Street. There was a canny feller drove the tatey waggon in every

129

I

Monday and Wednesday, and he would always look out for is and give's a lift. Rough and ready but a nice man all the same. Those are the best kind. I found that out a long time ago.

When I left O'Callaghan I didn't want to have nobody involved. But this day I bumped into Jim Kilcaldy, in the market, and he asks is where I was livin'. He kept on nosin' about so much I had to tell him. About leavin' O'Callaghan and everythin'. 'Thank God for that', he says. 'You couldn't be doing a better thing.' I says, 'It's all right for you sayin' that, Jim, but there's the bairns ye know. And we're at this place and it's a proper wreck. But I'm still goin' to live in it for the time bein' till we get somethin' better.' So he says, 'I'll come up and see you.' But I says, 'No, Jim. I don't want ye to know where I am and I don't want anybody else involved. I don't want anybody to say that I encouraged them to stick up for me.'

Well, he came up one Sunday all the same. He had been all over the shop lookin' for we. He had been to the bar, naturally, but had never thought of lookin' in the houses up at the back. But eventually he found out where we were. I had nothin' at all in the house but I said to him. 'Do ye want a cup of tea?'

'No, I'll have a pint in the bar, later,' he said. 'Have you got owt?'

I told him I didn't have a thing. And he says, 'Well, this is a fine kettle of fish, isn't it? Where's all your money?' Like everybody else, they all thought I had somethin'. I says, 'Well, Jim, what with him drinkin' it and pinchin' it, I'm down to the bones of me bum.' He says, 'There's half a dollar for you. It isn't much, but I'll come through the week and see you again.' And he did. He was a big daft feller. Always tellin' ye daft stories to make ye laugh no matter how depressed ye were. That's what I used to like about him. He could always make ye laugh.

Every day, after finishin' at the lodgin' house, I would go round all the property dealers in Shields seekin' for a better place for we to live in. And often I didn't get back till very late dependin' on whether I was lucky enough to get a lift back or not. It was a long up-hill walk home.

130

It was after eight o'clock when I got back one Thursday night. I was busy gettin' the bairns ready for bed and the door was open that looked down into the alley. I could hear the voices of the women in the shop across the road.

'She's a right brazen bitch is that one, you know, Mrs McArdle.'

'Don't tell me, Bella, I know. She's a real loose 'un that one. Our Tom said somebody saw her walkin' along the docks the other night.'

'Well, have you not seen her on the road, man. Every mornin' puttin' her thumb up to those dirty waggon drivers. She gets in with them as well. . . . With anybody. You don't need to be told what happens in there. They'll be takin' her into the pubs to do her pickin' up.'

'It's those poor little bairns I'm sorry for. Somebody should get the Cruelty man. They should be taken off her. I'll bet there's not one of them ever seen his father, or even know who he is for that matter.'

'No, you're right there, Mrs McArdle. What gets me is the way she walks about like Lady Muck always with her head stuck right up as though she owned the place. And those rooms not fit to keep a horse in.'

'A horse! I wouldn't even keep our Patch in there, and he's only a fox terrier.'

'She keeps that little one in bed all day. Goes out galavantin' and doesn't give a ha'penny tosser about him.'

All of a sudden me stomach heaved and I thought I was goin' to vomit. But there was nothin' in it to bring up. I sat meself down on the edge of the bed, and a queer feelin' came over is. I felt sort of dizzy, and these tiny lights was dancin' in front of me eyes. I lost the feelin' in me arms and I couldn't raise me hands. Me fingers was twitchin' funny-like and me whole body went cold and clammy. Me heart was beatin' like a machine-gun. Ratatattat. I took a deep breath, pulled meself together and stood up. Like somebody not right, I turned everythin' out and upside down. The kid's pockets, me purse. Umpteen times. Not a penny could I find. Then young Johnny came in.

131

'Johnny! Give's your tea money! Ye didn't spend it did ye? Well, where is it? I need it.'

'I'm sorry, Mother, but they went away and forgot it. But they'll give it to me tomorrow. Don't upset yourself, Ma. You shall have it. You don't pay the food bill today, do you? You've got tick till the weekend, and they'll always extend it. You're a good investment for them, Mother, and they know it.' Johnny was smilin'.

'C'mon, Ma, are the young 'uns in bed? I'll see to Walter, then we're going out. I'm going to take you for a nice walk. . . . Let's see your face, Ma. Give's a good look at you.'

Johnny took me face in his hands and turned it towards him.

'Mother, whatever's the matter? Are you all right? Sit down a while and I'll put a cup of tea on. We'll just stay in instead, and talk.'

'No, Johnny. No. I want to go out like ye said. I want to go for that walk.'

'Are you sure you're all right to go out, Ma. Like this?'

'I'm sure, son. I really want to go out with ye.'

'All right then, Mother. Come on now, everythin's goin' to be all right.'

Goin' out for the walk with Johnny was always a treat. When it was a fine night, the five of us would all go out together. Johnny carryin' Walter on his back as we trudged through the fields at the back of the Robin Hood, just walkin' and talkin' between worsel's. We would follow the rows of hedges all the way round and back. The kids used to play on the grass, and Johnny would always be tellin' how Joe and him had planned to save up enough money to buy is a marvellous business and a huge house already set up and just waitin' for somebody like me to go in and take the reins and be the big boss. Just like Mrs Robinson. They were savin' right now to buy is gowns and jewels as well, so they said. It would not be much longer to wait. I only had to be patient for a few more years till it would all come off for sure. I used to laugh and take a swipe at him. 'Get out of it, you silly bugger. Who do you think you're kiddin'? You're not the Prime Minister, ye know.

132

You're still only an office boy. But ye will be one day, son, stick in, ye will be. You'll be somebody important for your mother to be proud of and look up to. . . . But I couldn't be any more proud of ye no matter what ye done, than I am right now. And wor Joe, neither. He's a wild 'un, but I love him as well. Both of yous just the same.' And so it would go on, and by the time we got back, I would always be cheered, and we'd all be laughin' at his daft talk.

This particular night I really needed that walk, and so we went. As we were comin' across the last field I stopped him and told him what was on me mind.

'Johnny, I'm glad ye didn't have the tea money tonight. I'm really glad of it. God sent those fellers away without payin' ye tonight on purpose. I know he did. I was nearly goin' to do a very bad thing, tonight. I was goin' to wait until we were all abed, and then I was goin' to put the money in the meter and gas we all.'

'What? I don't believe it! I'll never believe it! You've got far too much spirit to do a thing like that, Ma. I've seen them bend your back, but they'll never break it. You must never say a thing like that again, or even let it enter your head. Has he been botherin' you again? If he has I'll kill him. Now, tonight! Was it him, Ma? Tell me!'

'No, it's got nothin' to do with O'Callaghan, son. It's them people downstairs.'

'What people, Mother?'

So I told him the whole story what had happened from the time I had come back from work that night.

'Come on, Mother. We're going to see them.'

We went over and Johnny knocked on the door and Mrs McArdle came out. She liked Johnny. He was always so neat and tidy and such a respectable lad. But as soon as she saw me standin' there as well, she slammed the door. Not so fast however, that Johnny's foot could not get in. The door jammed hard breakin' the sides of his poor bit boots. He quickly pushed open the door and pulled Mrs McArdle out.

'Is Mrs Manners and Mrs Johnson there as well? Well, they

can come out and listen to what I have to say. My mother is as good a woman as any of you! Probably better! And you people nearly made her put her head in the gas oven tonight! Maybe you would have done what she's done if you were in her shoes, and maybe you wouldn't! You probably couldn't even if you wanted to because it takes too much.' He then told them what had happened and what his mother had done for them, leavin' out about Jack O'Callaghan of course. That had nowt to do with them. After that he got a tight hold of me arm and marched is up the stairs to wor room.

From then onwards those gossipin' women couldn't do enough for we. Johnny would not have taken anythin' from them. Nothin' at all. However, I wasn't one to bear spite and I forgave them because I realised they had been thinkin' about the bairns. They had only had their interest at heart. These women then told all the neighbours of our situation and they all of them mucked in together to bring food, coal and cast-offs. However this couldn't last. I wanted nobody's charity. And the room was gettin' worse. I told the people we were leavin', and they begged is to stay.

'You don't need to worry about a thing, Mrs O'Callaghan. We'll see to your rent and everything. You need never want for anything if only you'll stay here where we can keep an eye on you.'

'I'm sorry, but I've made up me mind and that's that. Thank ye very much for bein' so kind to me and the bairns. But I can't bring them up properly here. I want somethin' better than this for my bairns.'

In 1932, me father died. He was eighty-three. He always felt he had a right to live to a ripe old age. One of his brothers had lived to ninety-three. And one, me Uncle Billy, lasted till he was ninety-seven. But me father died early through knockin' himself about too much with the drinkin' and the hard life he had led. It was his own fault though, and he couldn't blame nobody but heself for dyin' so young.

From the Robin Hood, we went to Eleanor Street. I rented

a small house there and I took in a young married couple as lodgers to help pay the rent. It might not have been the poshest place in the world but decent, clean livin' people lived there aside us, and it wasn't nearly so far to tramp to work.

In 1933 we got a council house in Thames Lane and we were quite content there. In fact those were the happiest days we ever had. Johnny was doin' well at his job and fetchin' in a canny bit, and Joe was sendin' a pound a month from sea. Edmund had started workin' on the buildin's as a labourer to Harry, his cousin. With what little I had been able to save, I had opened a savin's account in young Francie's name. Just a little somethin' put aside, because, as she was the only girl in the family, she was the one who was goin' to need it most of all one day. It wasn't much ye know but it would be a start for when she grew up and got married. I suppose there must have been about four pound in the bank by the time O'Callaghan heard about it. Takin' young Francie out of school one day by tellin' the teacher that she was wanted urgently at home concernin' her mother, O'Callaghan had took her to the bank, made her sign on the dotted line and took out the whole lot. He gave her a shillin' and a pat on the head, and sent her on her way.

Not long after, the Corporation told O'Callaghan to make alterations to the Leighton Street property, like gettin' a roadway built and doin' up the outside. But he wouldn't or couldn't. So he was kicked out altogether. From then on he lived in rooms for the rest of his life. Always havin' to move on from place to place but never again with me.

He used to get at the bairns to ask me to have him back. Mainly wor soft Joe and little Francie. But never Johnny, mind. Never Johnny. But it wouldn't have mattered one iota if he'd got at the whole lot of them. This was between him and me. And I wouldn't dream of it. People used to come up to is and say he really loved me after all that. But even if he did, he was too late now. Everythin' was finished and there was no turnin' back.

135

16

When we were at Thames Lane I took stock of meself and realised I had nowt I could complain about. I wasn't earnin' regular money meself, but Johnny, Joe and Edmund were all grown up just about. Francie would soon be earnin' her keep and even Walter was bringin' in a few coppers doin' errand boy's jobs. O'Callaghan was out of the way. And everythin' was fine. All me bairns were healthy in mind and in body, and I couldn't ask for no more than that. They had plenty of spunk and I was proud of them.

In spite of what I did to try and stop him, Joe had come back from sea and started boxin' again. This time for money. Stoker Allan, who he called Uncle Ned, was always at him and so was his Uncle Geordie. The only one who could have stopped him was wor Johnny and he wouldn't either. That's the trouble, he loved boxin' even more than wor Joe. And he would follow him round all his fights. Him, Geordie and Stoker all shoutin' together in his corner. And Joe always had a huge gang of friends who would follow him anywhere, not just because of the boxin' but just because of him. They used to go round the pubs yellin' and singin' like they weren't right. Quite a few of them played musical instruments and Joe loved a sing-song and a bit of daft carry-on more than anythin'. Johnny said he was really good, and that they used to bill him as the 'Knockout Specialist'. But how he could make a boxer, I'll never know. I'll grant ye he was very well built and very strong as well. But compared with his dad, and what he used to do. . . . Gettin' up early, and goin' for runs, eatin' and drinkin' only what'd do him good. Goin' to bed at the proper time and all that sort of thing. All the trainin' Joe did, was singin', dancin' and drinkin'. And some nights he never went to bed at all. He had tried to get a job back at Redhead's shipyard but they wouldn't have him back. One time when he was lookin' for work, wor Edmund said he'd get him a job. Clever-dick Edmund. He'd been workin' as a joiner's apprentice and knew nowt and nobody. But to hear him talkin' ye'd think he knew everythin' and everybody. This particular day, he'd gone for a job at a buildin' site. The foreman said, 'Can ye build chimneys?' 'Why aye, man', says Edmund. 'Can I build chimneys? I've been buildin' them all me life, man.' 'All right, clever shite', says the foreman. 'Come back at seven o'clock on Monday mornin' and get started on that roof over there. We'll soon see just how good ye really are.'

So in he waltzes that Friday night, full of heself. What he was goin' to do and what he wasn't goin' to do, was nobody's business.

'Still out of work?' he says to wor Joe.

'Aye.'

'Well, why don't you come and see me, I'll soon fix ye up. You can be my labourer.'

'Go and lose yerself, ye cheeky little upstart, or I'll black both your eyes for ye.'

'No, I'm serious, Joe. I'll get meself in there on Monday and see the foreman about startin' you on the Tuesday.'

Edmund was so keen I went out and got him a full set of tools that he said he needed. And some for Joe as well. In all it cost me nearly two pound.

Well, come the Monday, he has a go at the chimneys like he was told. He put three up and before the day was out, the whole lot had fallen off and smashed to pieces on the ground. 'Course he was sacked straight away. And that was two pound down the drain. Mind, he was a plucky kid. Fine lookin' he was with his mass of curly hair. Gobby, and always lookin' for a fight. He was a proper little Irishman. Two things had made him especially tough. One was that his own father, O'Callaghan, had given him hidin's like no man ever thrashed a son. And the other was Joe and Johnny. When he'd been just a kid at school, he'd always be sendin' for wor Johnny or wor Joe whenever he got into trouble. And that was practically every day. In the finish, they said, 'Ye'll just have to stand up for yerself, Edmund.' And they taught him how to look after

137

heself with his own fists. After that he come on well. He couldn't bear for anybody to tell him what to do. Wor Johnny had been tellin' him off for somethin' he'd done or said to me and he come out with, 'Who the hell d'ye think you are, Johnny? You're not me father. And I'm as much a Robinson as you are any time. So put them up.'

'Oh shut up, Edmund, before you get yourself hurt.'

'C'mon big man, let's see how good ye really are!'

'Go away, sonny boy. I've warned you once. I won't warn you again.'

Just then, wor Joe steps in between them. Edmund had the meat carver pointin' at wor Johnny. And Joe, easy as ye like, turns his back on him and faces wor Johnny. And winks at him. Then he and Johnny burst out laughin' and Edmund jabs the knife in poor Joe's backside. Joe turns round and grabs a hold of wor Edmund as though he was goin' to lay him out, and they all start laughin'. And that was the end of it.

Little Walter wasn't like Johnny, Joe or Edmund. Even though he'd only be about nine or ten, ye could see he wouldn't make a boxer. It'd have showed long before then. He wanted nothin' to do with fightin'. And I was grateful for that. Even the other lads couldn't push him into it. Mind ye, it certainly wasn't 'cos he was too soft. When he was only eight he had slashed his arm on a barrel brace and he never even cried. The metal spring had made a gash that must have been six inches long at the least. And gapin' to the bone. There was bits of rusty metal had got right down into it and I had to scrape them out with a spoon so it wouldn't get poisoned. All the time I was doin' this and puttin' antiseptic in it, he never said one word. He just stood near the window with his arm on the table readin' his Dandy comic. He was an awful one for his comics. He spent all his pocket money on them, what little he had. He used to deliver papers and the man in the shop would give him last week's left-overs. And then he'd swap them with his pals. If only he'd have set his mind to read some of Johnny's knowledge books. They'd have done him a lot more good. But like all of them, all except Joe that is, he was stubborn as an old mule.

By 1934, Joe was away at sea again and Johnny had started courtin' this shy lass from Tyne Dock. She was called Evelyn Smithwhite and Johnny had met her at a cyclin' club do. Johnny was keen on cyclin' like he was on anythin' that kept him fit. He was daft about it. And he was daft about her too. He even bought her a bike even though she didn't know how to work the pedals properly.

A Ladies' Hercules is what they called it. He was really pleased with heself when he got it. They had went to Barnard Castle for one of the cyclin' club's meetin's, and Johnny had to keep one hand on his handlebars and the other one on Evelyn's saddle and steer her all the way there. When he got there on the Saturday night, a telegram came to him from wor Joe sayin' that he'd just got back from sea. Evelyn couldn't ride back herself and Johnny wanted to get back as fast as he could. So he left her there with the rest of the camp sayin' he'd be back on the Monday for her. Which he was of course.

We'd all been very anxious about Joe that trip because so much had happened to him. Somewhere abroad, Durban I think it was, he'd picked up dysentery and had to go into hospital. Then, when he'd got heself put right again, he caught a ship goin' to Russia. Him and a couple of his mates had gone to this dance at a place called Vladivostok. He'd got into an argument and the bouncers had jumped on him. A big fight had started and in next to no time all the Russians were on to wor Joe. They got him down these stairs and were kickin' hell's bells out of him when this Welsh crew from his sister ship came in. He reckoned that saved his life. I think it was the SS Goodwood he was on when they crashed into an iceberg in the Atlantic and got stuck there. Part of the front of the ship had caved in and the only way they could get it freed and on their way again, was for some of the crew to climb overboard to repair the damage. Wor Joe had been amongst them. And to keep them goin', they were lowerin' bottles of rum to them. It was in all the papers at the time. Naturally we'd all been worried about Joe. So ye can see why wor Johnny left Evelyn in Barnard Castle to come straight home.

17

In 1935 Johnny got engaged to Evelyn Smithwhite and with all the other bairns growin' up, he was set on me havin' somethin' to occupy me mind and to provide for the future. There was a lot of unemployment and times were gettin' hard again.

'You must get a place of your own, Mother, to keep the wolf from the door. Some little business so you can keep your self-respect and be sure of a steady income. It need only be something small that you could easily handle. I'll give you all the help I can and I'll see the rest of them pull their weight too.'

By and by, a little shop in William Street came up for sale. I had yearned for this little shop for a long while. It was a small general dealer's in a poor but busy area. And poor people make good customers. They can't always pay on the dot, but they're honest if ye trust them. And they can never be bothered to shop around. If they know where they can get all they want handy, then that's where they'll go. They like a place where they can come in drunk and know you'll give them the stuff they want even if they've forgot what they've come in for. They want a place they can come into with their curlers in or in their slippers and dressin' gowns. They know ye aren't goin' to diddle them by bamboozlin' their little bairns if they send them in with a message. They like to know that when ye say ye haven't got so and so, that ye really haven't got it. But if you say, 'I'll get it by such and such a time', that you'll get it by such and such a time. And that's the way it was with me. I asked the owner of the shop how much he wanted for it.

'Forty-five pounds.'

'Forty-five pound! That's an awful lot, isn't it? Ye haven't got much stock, so ye can't have much business. Can I look in your bins? These is goin' mouldy. Ye cannot sell it in that state. They'd get food-poisonin' man. I'm offerin' thirty-two pound. Not a single farthin' more. I'll be back tomorrow mornin' for your answer.'

He argued and argued. But I'd made up me mind and that was that. On the Sunday the business changed hands for thirty-two pound. By Monday we were all at it. First we chucked out all the old stock. Then we cleaned and polished all the fittin's and scrubbed the place out from top to bottom. The shop and the rooms that went with it. There were two bedrooms upstairs, and downstairs there was a livin' room with a big fireplace and an oven. Scarcely was it dry, before it was thoroughly painted. As soon as we got started we saw what we were in for. It was in a shockin' mess. Things might look all right from the outside, but when ye see beneath the surface it's amazin' what muck ye find. At one time, there had been a bakery next door, and when we pulled off the wallpaper in the livin' room, the beetles poured out like a waterfall. With black 'uns and brown 'uns. Cockroaches and spiders and all sorts. Ye couldn't step on the floor without squashin' dozens of them with a horrible cracklin' and squelshin'. Noises in the walls was somethin' I found out later that I would just have to put up with. Ye used to try and guess if they were rats or beetles. They both made the same noise, and we had plenty of both.

I worked it out in me mind that I was goin' to sell a little bit of everythin'. I was sufficiently well known to get credit, and so by the end of the week, me little shop was fully stocked. All your main groceries and all the little bits of things that would attract customers. Anythin' and everythin' that would give is a quick turnover. All kinds of tabs (cigarettes), baccy and matches for the men. All kinds of sweets for the kids. Seasonin's for the dinner table like nutmeg, peppers, salts and cheap spices. Pans and kettles. Knives and spoons. Hankies and dishcloths. Soap and toothbrushes. Pipes and firelighters. Hairnets and stockin's. Tea-cosies and toys. Snuff and bait-cans. Combs and shovels. Plasters and bootlaces, liver pills and lipstick. Woodbines, I would sell in ones and twos. A penny for a Wills Woodie and two matches to go with it in case one went out, would draw the men in. A business on these lines in that area, and in those times, couldn't fail. And it didn't. Long before the first week was out, I was takin' three pound a day. Folks saw what was goin' in and they came to buy. They would knock on

141

the door at yon time at night when other shops were long since closed.

'Missus O'Callaghan, ha' ye got some belly-ache pills? Me man's bad with the beer.'

'Can ye spare is half a pound o' lentils for the broth I'm makin? I forgot to get any, and. . . .'

'Gis five tabs will ye, hinny? I'm reet out on 'em and I'm dyin' for a smoke.'

'I've got to put wor lad's bait up and I haven't a crust of bread in the hoose at all.'

Soon I was changin' me sweet windows three times a week. And that's a good sign. I sold an awful lot of sweets. Ha'penny gob-stoppers, lickrish, cinnamon, dolly mixtures, all them things. I really knew nowt about that kind of business, but I'd tackle anythin'. People would say tiv is, 'Hey, Missus, if ye put shit in your winder, ye would surely sell it.'

When the travellers came in, maybe just for a packet of tabs or an ounce of St Bruno, I'd say, 'Hey, you've got the writin' place, haven't ye. Gis a few packets of pins and some envelopes and pads. I'll sell them, I bet ye.' 'Course, I would sing with the customers, and all that. Anythin' to keep them happy and make them come back to my little shop. Things like, 'Just look at my lovely hair, hinny, How d'ye think I got that? Well, it was them curlers that did it. They're only tuppence a packet.' Or, 'Howay, me bonny lass, look what I've got for ye.' And I would rhyme it off so they laughed and were pleased. 'How about a new kettle for ye, Mrs Nicholson? Make a lovely cup of tea. I use one mesel'. Lovely mastin' they give ye.'

'Well I would, but I haven't got the money. . . . They polish up nice though don't they?'

'Look pet, tek it. It'll only cost ye a tanner a week.'

Sometimes they would come in for a special brand of baccy I'd never heard of. So I'd tell them I had just sold out on it. 'D'ye smoke much of it. . . ? Oh d'ye? How much a week would ye say. . . ? Right. Come back in an hour's time and I'll have plenty. I'll put in a regular order for ye so ye can come and collect it, and you'll know I'll always have it put by for ye.'

142

Then I'd run 'round to the wholesaler's and get it for when the poor bloke came back.

Snuff? I could sell it by the ton. That, and clay pipes. Women were the worst for the snuff. I had like a little spoon thing. Two measures. . . . Heaped, or level, dependin' on what they wanted. Ye learned to give a special little tap against the side so they got the proper amount. I learned to scoop so they were satisfied without gettin' too much. It was very expensive and ye couldn't afford to spill any. Fourpence ha'penny for a little wee bit, and a tanner for a heaped-up spoonful. One woman had three bobs' worth a day for to clear her brain.

Staples like tateys and bread and milk sold very well. To satisfy the Health people's rules and regulations, your milk couldn't be divided up inside the shop. The urns had to be carried outside and ladled in the street. Milk was normally stored in open marble dishes where it could collect dust. I knew the idea was to keep the germs away but some of the things they made ye do were so silly ye wouldn't credit it. They brought pressures to bear on sanitary inspectors and they passed them on to us little traders. But the big concerns could buy and sell the inspectors just like they can today. Eventually I was stopped from sellin' milk altogether. But that didn't matter too much because I was doin' so well with everythin' else.

18

Young Francie was now about sixteen or seventeen, and she was helpin' is in the shop. But I found I could manage on me own now, and she wanted to work somewhere else and make her own way. I had no quarrel with that. They had to be independent sooner or later. So she went to Marks & Spencer's over the Christmas and then down to Bayswater in London to work as a chambermaid at a hotel. She stayed there for three months and then her and this Irish lass she'd got pally with ran away. All this time and I never had a single letter from her. I wasn't too happy in the first place goin' all that way to a big city. Specially with her bein' so young and so bonny. I feared somethin' had happened to her so I went to the police. The trouble was they didn't like livin' at the hotel because of all the rules and regulations. So they'd got a room in Camden Town between them while they looked for another job.

They got one after a week, at the Cumberland Hotel. Francie had made a friend of the chef at the other place they'd been workin' at, and he lent them an alarm clock. They couldn't afford to buy one and they were frightened in case they wouldn't wake up in time to start work in the mornin'. They had to be up at half past five. Francie had asked the chef to set it for them because they didn't know how to work it. So he set it for half past five and wound it up. On the way back from the chef's at Bayswater, the clock went off. The three of them must have been wooden because at the time they set it, it was still in the middle of the afternoon. So it went off at half past five at night instead. Francie was walkin' through the crowded streets with it ringin' away like all the bells in hell. She hadn't the savvy to switch it off and was tryin' to muffle it under her coat, when these two big coppers came up to her. They asked her her name and took her back to her lodgin's. They sat her down and said, 'Do you know we could put you on the next train and send you back to South Shields? You haven't written to your mother for seven weeks. You should be ashamed of yourself. Your poor mother must be worried out of her mind.' So young Francie had told them she was sorry and that she'd got a new good job and promised to write is.

'You bet you will, girl. Go and get a pen and paper and write a letter right now, while we are here. We'll post it for you.'

That night the 'tecs came to William Street and told is that me bairn was all right and in good hands. Apparently the hotel she was workin' at had a good name. So ye see, the police can be all right. They were always kind to me, in all my dealin's with them.

However, after young Francie had been at the Cumberland Hotel for a while, she left to work as a barmaid in Battersea.

Then she stopped writin' again. Not that she'd written very often anyway. But it had stopped altogether for four months. I got wor Edmund to telephone to her and tell her I was very poorly and that she had to come home at once. That was the only thing that would have made her. I was waitin' for her at the station.

'Right, my girl. You're home for good now and you're not goin' anywhere no more. I don't care how good the job is.'

Francie was the favourite with all my lads. And I think with all the boys for miles around. Johnny and Edmund were strict with her and tried to protect her too much. But Joe was different. Although he would always be concerned about her as well, he was much easier on her. Johnny and Edmund didn't go much to the pubs. Anyway they were both courtin' strong.

Johnny with his lass Evelyn, and Edmund with a smashin' colleen, Nellie Curran. But no lass could tie our Joe down. He just didn't care. As long as he had all his mates around, he was happy. I think he enjoyed a street fight in some foreign port with all his sailor pals as much as a proper boxin' match in a fightin' ring. Him and his mates would go round to the pubs in Shields. And the rougher they were, the better he liked it. He always made it his business to call in at the bar where Francie was workin' at the time. She worked in umpteen places. She could never hold a job down for very long. Always wantin' to try somethin' new. Joe would go in to see Francie was all right, have a couple of beers, and be off somewhere else. But most nights, especially Saturdays, he'd end up at wor Francie's bar to see her home. If she told him to go home heself because she had a feller that was goin' to see her home, Joe would ask who he was and then go over and look this feller over. One night, Joe was gettin' heself spruced up ready to go out when Francie says to him. 'I don't know what to do with meself, Joe. I've got so many boyfriends. I don't know which one to go out with.'

'How like? What d'ye mean, Francie?'

'Well, like tonight. I've got three separate dates with three different lads.'

'Well, what'll ye do if they all come to the door at once?'

'They're not all comin' to the house, you silly bugger. What

145

do ye take me for? Do ye think I'm daft or something? I've arranged to meet them at different places.'

'Like where though, Francie? Near here, ye mean?'

'Why, of course. I'm not going to tramp all over town to meet some bloke. They have to come and seek me. One I'm supposed to be meetin' outside Ropper's fish-and-chip shop, another one under the big lamp, and the other outside St Bede's Church.'

So while all this is goin' on, I'm sayin' nowt. Just gettin' about me business as though I'm payin' no attention to what the two of them's talkin' about. Joe carries on polishin' his shoes till they're sparklin', whistlin' away to heself.

'Tata, Ma', he says. 'See you later on, Francie.'

'Tata, Joe. Ye big daft bugger.'

In twenty minutes he's back again. There's a knock on the door and Joe pushes in three fellers. They didn't know what to do with theirsel's.

'Here you are, Francie', says wor Joe. He lines these three poor fellers up under the light.

'Now, get a good look at them, and take your choice.'

He goes out whistlin' and ye could hear him laughin' to heself all the way up the street. Poor Francie. She ran upstairs to her bedroom cryin' her eyes out and stayed in all that night.

I made these three fellers a cuppa tea and sent them on their way.

Whenever Joe was short of a few bob for a beer, he'd walk up and down the shop all dressed up. I'd say to him, 'I know what you're after, Joe, but you're not gettin' a ha'penny out of me. You should have made your money last instead of spendin' it as though ye thought it was the last day on earth.'

I'd go back in and sit meself down to do a bit of darnin'. A few minutes later he would come in. Poor bugger. He knew he had no money to go out with, but still he would get heself ready. And never a night would he stay in.

Then he'd come and sit opposite is at the table and start makin' these daft faces of his. 'Go way, wor Joe, before I clout ye.'

146

'Why, Ma? Why? I've only come to sit and look at the most beautiful girl under the sun. There's nothin' wrong with that, is there?'

I'd keep him waitin' like that for half an hour or so until I could see his patience was gettin' the better of him. He'd get up.

'Well, I might as well take me coat off and just go to bed.'

'Yes, ye might as well, Joe. You think money grows on trees. Well it doesn't. And the sooner ye realise that, the better it'll be for ye.'

Then he'd start a bit of shadow boxin' and start knockin' the fly paper all over the room.

'Stoppit, wor Joe, or I'll let ye have it, mind. I've warned ye.'

'Ye wouldn't raise your hand against your poor defenceless son, would ye, Ma?'

'Yes, I would.'

'I've changed me mind. I think I'll stay in and tantalise you instead.'

Then he'd start with his daft faces again. He'd see he was gettin' nowhere so out into the shop he'd go.

'Why don't ye sell beer, Ma, instead of all this junk? Who in his right mind wants snuff and nutmegs and all that stuff.'

'Because you'd drink is out of house and home. That's why.'

Then all'd be quiet for a while and so I would go into the shop. It was all dark, and I couldn't see him. All of a sudden he'd jump out and grab is from behind and give is a kiss.

'If I catch you at that till, Joe, I'll nail your hand to the counter.' I'd pick up the hammer I used to crack the toffee with, and wave it at him.

'I'll rive your liver out by the roots!'

'One day, they'll have ye for the way you've treated me, Ma. And ye know what I'll say? I'll say, "Forgive that poor woman, judge. How was she to know that I was a saint disguised as the devil?" '

'Here! Here's five bob. Get to hell out of here, and don't come back. And when ye do, make sure ye don't wake me up!'

147

Whenever our Johnny was in, Joe would always get round him. Much easier than he'd get round me. With Johnny ye always had to say the right and proper things and do the right and proper things. And always dress the part. He didn't like ye to make a fool of yourself. But did Joe care? Did he hell. He played on it. He was twice the size of wor Johnny, so he would go upstairs and deliberately put Johnny's jacket on which only came half way up his arms. Then he'd mebbes blacken his face with soot and put all Johnny's ties round his neck. Then he'd take off his trousers and come down in his underpants with a straight face.

'Right, Johnny. I'll tell ye what I'll do. If ye give is threepence, I'll walk round the block like this.'

'Don't be so daft, Joe. What'll the neighbours think? It'll embarrass my mother. It can only affect the business if you do things like that. Howay, man. Act your age and think about our mother.'

'Rightio then, Johnny. If ye don't give's ten bob, I'm not only goin' round the block, I'm goin' to sing dirty songs as well while I'm at it. And then I'm goin' to the market-place and I'm goin' to shout as loud as I can that me Ma's got rats in the shop. And that all the customers get, is what the rats don't want.'

What could ye do? Johnny'd give him a few bob and then Joe'd be upstairs in a jiffy, get ready and come bouncin' back.

'I wouldn't have really done it, ye know Johnny. I love ye, don't I, Ma? I'm her real favourite, Johnny. She knows I'm the true, loyal one.'

After a voyage he'd be dafter than ever. When his ship docked in the Tyne, he would come home with at least a dozen of his shipmates.

'Howay, lads, come and see me Ma! She'd love to see yous all.'

'Oh no Joe! Not again. Why don't ye come and see your mother by yerself, ye no good, lazy lout?'

'They've all been dyin' to see ye, Ma. I've told them all about ye. This lot have been waitin' to get back to Shields ever since we left Durban, when I told them about the great

148

welcome we'd all get. Put the flags up, Ma! Where's the bloody flags? Ye knew we'd be back this month. Come on fellers, in ye get. Make yersel's at home. That's Willy over there, Ma. The one with the big gob. Put those crates over there, lads. Get the glasses, Ma. I've got somethin' extra special for you all the way from Istanbul. . . . There, now. That'll do ye good. Drink that.'

'What? A bottle of stout from Istanbul? Wor Joe, ye'd say owt but your prayers! Ye must think me as daft as you are.'

'Aye, but that's no ordinary Guinness, Ma. That's special stuff, isn't it, boys? That's what the harem girls drink. Puts fire in their bellies for the dancin' and all that. Howay Ma, gis a dance! Me mother's a marvellous dancer, lads. Gan on, have a dance with her. No, me first! Me first, Ma . . . tra la la! Now then, isn't she great, lads?'

'Get yersel' lost, ye daft nowt. Gan on wi' ye. Ye cannot dance at all and ye never could. Ye big, flat-footed fool, ye.'

'Pay no notice, lads. She's pullin' your legs. Howay Mother, I'm goin' to learn ye a new waltz I picked up while I was away. . . . No, Ma you're doin' it all wrong. Watch me. . . . Watch, Ma! Just follow my dainty steps. . . . De de dedada. . . . That's good. . . . That's champion. See. What did I tell you boys? Ye can go round the whole world a thousand times, but ye'll never find a one like me old Ma. Will they, Ma? Hey, gis a kiss.'

Night after night was the same thing, and usually the same crowd. After the pubs had closed, they would all troop in singin' and laughin', bangin' and fallin' about. Joe thought there was nothin' I liked better. When he came in, he always took the place over.

'Gan into the shop, Dick, and pull down the biggest ham ye can find. Me mother'll show ye how to slice it. . . . No, wait a minute. Leave her to enjoy hersel' with the dancin'. I'll do it. . . . Ma! How d'ye work this bloody stupid thing? It's bust again! Never mind. I've found the big knife. . . . Now . . . right Jem, cut those loaves up and Scotty can make the sandwiches. . . . It's all right, Ma, I know it's from the shop. Don't worry! This is really good business for ye. . . . We're goin' to have a real feed tonight. And me mother's going to sing to yous all. She's got the most beautiful voice in the world. Wait till ye hear her sing "Kathleen". Howay, Ma! Sing "Kathleen". We're all waitin' on ye. "I'll take you home again. . . ." '

After they had all gone, which would never be before mornin', I used to tell Joe that I had had enough. But I might as well have saved me breath, it was no use at all talkin' to him and tryin' to get him to see sense.

'No more, Joe! D'ye hear me? No more! Those boozy pals of yours make a hell of a mess. Broken bottles . . . and all that din. . . . The neighbours'll have the police round before long. They'll think I'm keepin' a bedlam house with your crazy lot. If ye bring anybody else in, I'll flatten the lot of yous.'

'All right, Ma. I promise. I know they were a bit rough last night, but that's the finish, I promise ye. No more. Just you and me from now on. No drinkin'. Just a quiet chat between worsel's, eh?'

That night, and every other night that Joe was back, the whole crowd would come burstin' in again. First Joe would tell them all to be dead quiet and hide around the corner out of sight. Then he would tap on the door.

'It's only me, Ma. It's just me, Joe, your favourite son. The gentle, friendly one who loves his Ma the best.'

'Are ye sure you've got nobody else with ye? I can hear somebody laughin' out there!'

'No, Ma, honest. That's just some drunken fool down the street. Nowt to do with me, Ma. Open up, Ma. It's freezin' out here. You'll soon sharp see if I'm tellin' the truth or not.'

As soon as he heard the bolt bein' drawn back, Joe would wave to his mates who would all gather at the door. And as soon as I opened it, they would all rush in, led by Joe.

'Get out! Get out, ye bloody waster! I told ye not to fetch anybody back here again. I'm too tired. I want to go to bed.'

'We won't make any noise, Ma. We'll just sing quietly. No dancin' tonight. We'll just play cards. No singin' either. I promise.'

I'd bray him with anythin' that came to hand. A broom, a